# TEST PREPARATION *and* INSTRUCTIONAL STRATEGIES GUIDE *for*
# INTELLIGENCE-LED POLICING

Leadership, Strategies & Tactics

THOMAS E. BAKER

43-08 162nd Street
Flushing, NY 11358
www.LooseleafLaw.com
800-647-5547

This publication is not intended to replace nor be a substitute for any official procedural material issued by your agency of employment nor other official source. Looseleaf Law Publications, Inc., the author and any associated advisors have made all possible efforts to ensure the accuracy and thoroughness of the information provided herein but accept no liability whatsoever for injury, legal action or other adverse results following the application or adoption of the information contained in this book.

©2009 by Looseleaf Law Publications, Inc. All rights reserved. No part of this book may be reproduced, stored in a retrieval system, or transcribed, in any form or by any means, electronic, mechanical, photocopying, recording, or otherwise, without the prior written permission of the Copyright owner.

For such permission, contact Looseleaf Law Publications, Inc., 43-08 162nd Street, Flushing, New York 11358, (800) 647-5547, www.LooseleafLaw.com.

---

This publication is intended for use with
INTELLIGENCE-LED POLICING
*Leadership, Strategies and Tactics*
by
Thomas E. Baker
ISBN 978-1-932777-75-8 – 370 Pages – Softcover
To order a copy of this book, additional copies of this test guide
or a free catalog, contact us.
Toll-free (800) 647-5547
Fax (718) 539-0941
www.LooseleafLaw.com

---

**Attention Instructors - PowerPoint Presentation Available**

To assist you in preparing a seminar based on "Intelligence-led Policing: Leadership Strategies and Tactics," a PowerPoint Presentation is available upon request.

# Table of Contents

Introduction: A Career Journey .................................................. 1

## PART I  INSTRUCTIONAL CONTENT .............................................. 5

### Prologue: Critical Thinking and the Intelligence Analyst .......... 7
- Synopsis .................................................................. 7
- Learning Objectives ....................................................... 9
  - Prologue - Questions ................................................... 11

### Chapter 1  Introduction .................................................. 13
- Synopsis ................................................................. 13
- Learning Objectives ...................................................... 14
  - Chapter 1 - Questions .................................................. 15
- Chapter 1 Focus Concepts ................................................. 17

### Chapter 2  Organizational Strategies ..................................... 19
- Synopsis ................................................................. 19
- Learning Objectives ...................................................... 20
  - Chapter 2 - Questions .................................................. 21
- Chapter 2 Focus Concepts ................................................. 23

### Chapter 3  Crime Analysis Strategies ..................................... 25
- Synopsis ................................................................. 25
- Learning Objectives ...................................................... 27
  - Chapter 3 - Questions .................................................. 28
- Chapter 3 Focus Concepts ................................................. 31

### Chapter 4  CompStat Integration .......................................... 33
- Synopsis ................................................................. 33
- Learning Objectives ...................................................... 34
  - Chapter 4 - Questions .................................................. 35
- Chapter 4 Focus Concepts ................................................. 37

## PART II  STRATEGIC LEADERSHIP ............................................. 39

### Chapter 5  Strategic Leadership and Communication ................... 41
- Synopsis ................................................................. 41
- Learning Objectives ...................................................... 43
  - Chapter 5 - Questions .................................................. 43
- Chapter 5 Focus Concepts ................................................. 46

**Chapter 6   Leadership Planning** ..................................................... 47
　Synopsis ........................................................................................ 47
　Learning Objectives ...................................................................... 49
　　　Chapter 6 - Questions ............................................................ 50
　Chapter 6 Focus Concepts ............................................................ 53

**Chapter 7   Analytical Products** ...................................................... 55
　Synopsis ........................................................................................ 55
　Learning Objectives ...................................................................... 56
　　　Chapter 7 - Questions ............................................................ 57
　Chapter 7 Focus Concepts ............................................................ 60

**PART III   TACTICAL APPLICATIONS** .......................................... 61

**Chapter 8   Analytical Models and Charting** ................................... 63
　Synopsis ........................................................................................ 63
　Learning Objectives ...................................................................... 65
　　　Chapter 8 - Questions ............................................................ 66
　Chapter 8 Focus Concepts ............................................................ 69

**Chapter 9   Investigative Strategies** ................................................. 71
　Synopsis ........................................................................................ 71
　Learning Objectives ...................................................................... 72
　　　Chapter 9 - Questions ............................................................ 73
　Chapter 9 Focus Concepts ............................................................ 76

**Chapter 10   Tactical Leadership: Training** ..................................... 77
　Synopsis ........................................................................................ 77
　Learning Objectives ...................................................................... 79
　　　Chapter 10 - Questions .......................................................... 80
　Chapter 10 Focus Concepts .......................................................... 82

**Epilogue   Concluding Focus Points** ................................................ 83
　Synopsis ........................................................................................ 83
　Learning Objectives ...................................................................... 84
　　　Epilogue - Questions .............................................................. 84
　Epilogue Focus Concepts .............................................................. 87
　Conclusion .................................................................................... 88

## PART IV  INSTRUCTIONAL CONTENT ........ 89

### Instructor Segment ........ 91
- Instructor Guide Content ........ 91
- Instruction/Curriculum ........ 92
- Instructional Strategies ........ 93
- Case Study Method Applications ........ 93
- Practical Exercise: Prologue ........ 93
- Practical Exercise: Chapter 1 ........ 94
- Practical Exercise: Chapter 2 ........ 94
- Practical Exercise: Chapter 3 ........ 95
- Practical Exercise: Chapter 4 ........ 95
- Practical Exercise: Chapter 5 ........ 96
- Practical Exercise: Chapter 6 ........ 96
- Practical Exercise: Chapter 7 ........ 97
- Practical Exercise: Chapter 8 ........ 97
- Practical Exercise: Chapter 9 ........ 98
- Practical Exercise: Chapter 10 ........ 98
- Practical Exercise: Epilogue ........ 99
- Conclusion ........ 99

### Appendix A  Seminar: Intelligence-led Policing ........ 101
- Seminar Description ........ 101
- Textbook ........ 102
- Course Objectives ........ 102
- Seminar Methods ........ 102
   - Progression 1: The Case Study Method ........ 102
   - Progression 2: Master Intelligence Concepts ........ 103
   - Progression 3: Critical Thinking ........ 103
   - Progression 4: Follow-Up ........ 103
- Teaching Philosophy ........ 104
- Learning Instruction ........ 104
- Evaluation and Learning Process ........ 104
- Attendance ........ 105
- Course Requirements ........ 106
- Teaching Philosophy ........ 107
- Seminar Outline – Learning Objectives and Practical Exercises ........ 107
   - A.  PROLOGUE: CRITICAL THINKING AND THE INTELLIGENCE ANALYST ........ 107

    B. CHAPTER 1: INTELLIGENCE-LED POLICING .......... 108
    C. CHAPTER 2: ORGANIZATIONAL STRATEGIES ....... 109
    D. CHAPTER 3: CRIME ANALYSIS STRATEGIES .......... 111
    E. CHAPTER 4: COMPSTAT OPERATIONS .................. 112
    F. CHAPTER 5: STRATEGIC LEADERSHIP AND
       COMMUNICATION ........................................................ 113
    G. CHAPTER 6: LEADERSHIP AND PLANNING ............ 114
    H. CHAPTER 7: ANALYTICAL PRODUCTS ..................... 115
    I. CHAPTER 8: ANALYTICAL MODELS AND
       CHARTING .................................................................... 117
    J. CHAPTER 9: INVESTIGATIVE STRATEGIES ............. 118
    K. CHAPTER 10: TACTICAL LEADERSHIP TRAINING 119
    L. EPILOGUE: TEN INTELLIGENCE-LED POLICING
       STRATEGIES ................................................................. 121
  Conclusion ............................................................................... 122

Appendix B   Fill in the Blank Questions - Answer Key ............ 123

Appendix C   Multiple Choice Questions - Answer Key ............ 129

Appendix D   Critical Thinking Essay Questions ......................... 131

Appendix E   ILP Instructor: Critical Thinking Exam ................. 133
  ANSWER SOLUTION KEY ............................................................ 136

# INTRODUCTION: A CAREER JOURNEY

*Always let your character and badge shine everywhere, sustain the effort, with perseverance, and determination. When you think it is impossible to continue the struggle, think critically, problem solve, and double the effort.*

— Tom Baker

*Intelligence-Led Policing: Instructional Strategies and Promotional Guide* serves as a sourcebook on your voyage for understanding Intelligence-Led Policing. The learning guide supports *Intelligence-Led Policing: Leadership, Strategies, and Tactics* and serves as an interactive learning tool.

The purpose is to summarize key concepts that are more difficult to apply, and emphasize understanding, test-taking applications, and information retention.

An important journey question persists for every officer: Where is my career going? Answering this question means defining your path goals, and objectives. Personal goals and objectives keep careers on track to reach proper destinations.

Police officer responsibilities require flexibility, preparedness, and a call to duty. Successful careers start with a road map for arriving at destinations on time. You have started on the right path by reading the Intelligence-Led Policing book and study guide.

This is your personal journey; make the most of life, and prepare for your future now.

As described in *Effective Police Leadership: Moving Beyond Management*, learning is an interactive, not passive experience:

"*Those who prepare for leadership study the position, rather than memorize promotional examination questions. Potential leaders with knowledge and expertise achieve success on examinations. Awareness of professional requirements allows candidates to reason examination questions. Preparing for the role assures success on the examination, interview, and police assessment process."*

Those who desire to be successful "can do" leaders in the twenty-first century must prepare now. "Can do" leaders read leadership materials such as those contained in this book, and take every opportunity to keep pace with the future. They anticipate and prepare for leadership positions that may become available.

*Intelligence-Led Policing* will help you develop "can do" leadership skills. Keep this book and reread it for understanding rather than memorization. *Intelligence-Led Policing* will help you focus on your career as a police leader and arrive at your professional destination.

Continue to read and prepare for leadership roles during the course of your career. Apply ILP concepts to the following practical exercises, which will help retain pertinent concepts, as you prepare for future leadership responsibilities.

The basic theme of this guide concerns the development of study skills necessary to succeed at advancing police careers, and test-taking skills for promotion examinations.

Learning is a lifetime process; the essence is human growth and development. There are many ways to learn; field practice components provide essential learning feedback and applications. Reading, study, and research assist in realizing the officer's potential.

Police officers require intellectual stimulation for future leadership preparation and responsibilities. Mental agility provides the foundation for effective decision-making at every command level.

The street is one dimension of police culture. Officers fit for command think on many levels of analysis. Achieving this task requires taking the high road, reaching beyond your initial grasp, and exceeding your reach.

Human growth and development requires exceeding one's imagination and believing in your dream of success.

Officers can easily recognize competent leaders and are standing by to follow well-prepared commanders and supervisors. This book and supplement text will help future leaders arrive on time and meet their career destination requirements.

4

# PART I
## INSTRUCTIONAL CONTENT

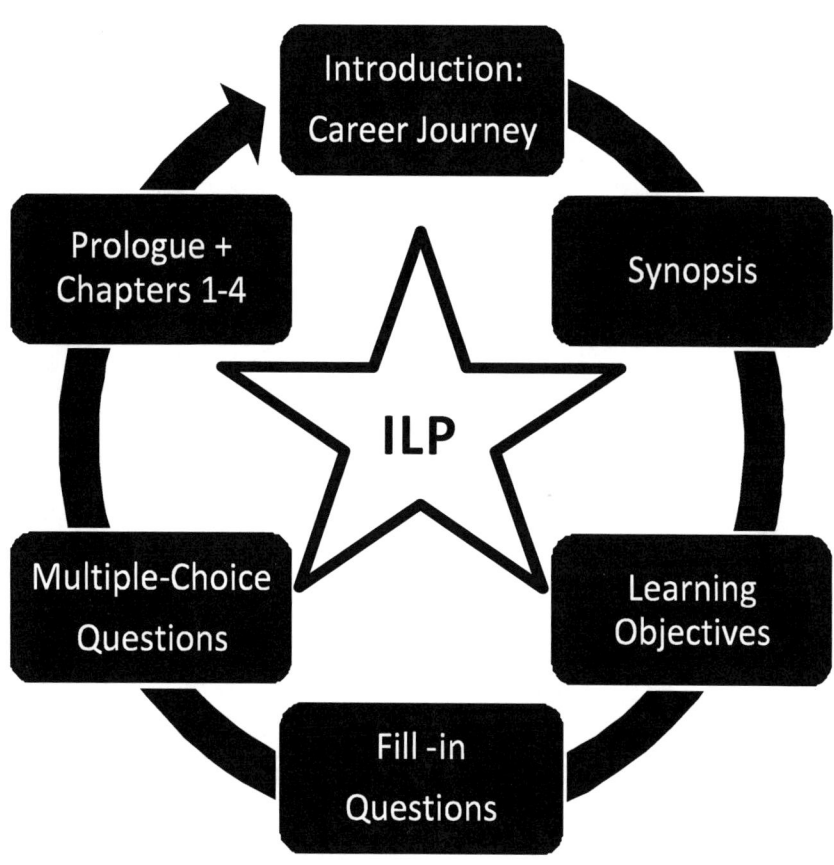

# Prologue: Critical Thinking and the Intelligence Analyst

## Synopsis

The analyst's role requires multi-tasking and thriving performance in a rapidly changing environment. The new role under the ILP philosophy suggests escalating responsibilities and collaboration throughout law enforcement agencies. Coordination requirements with commanders, middle managers, sergeants, officers, and detectives have increased considerably.

Critical thinking skills are essential intelligence analyst proficiencies, concepts difficult to define. Critical thinking concepts offer great promise, even with definition limitations.

Successful intelligence training stresses critical thinking skills as vital field components. Moreover, ILP requires analytical capabilities.

This leadership style is concerned with a few conceptual decisions that have maximum impact on the intervention, and prevention of criminal activities.

The executive decision-making process revolves around the ILP management model, and strategic critical thinking. The goal is to develop an organizational and community vision, which targets crime with maximum personnel and logistical resources.

The concept of vision applies to law intelligence analysis, strategic and tactical planning. Commanders, middle managers, and first-line supervisors require intelligence analysis to enhance leadership decision-making.

Vision, strategic and tactical planning remain core requirements for police leaders.

Critical thinking, intelligence, and crime analysis provide direction. Leaders supply officers with a map and compass for getting there.

Intelligence analysis assists in answering basic direction questions: *Where is the law enforcement agency going? How will the law enforcement agency get there, assess, and evaluate its arrival?*

Intelligence-led policing and intelligence analysis is the primary method for the development of vision, to execute meaningful future-oriented decisions.

Accurate intelligence analysis ensures that valid and reliable criminal intelligence serves as the foundation for plotting the department's future course. The key to establishing vision and strategic planning is the ILP analysis process.

ILP helps chart the course, defines strategic goals, and assists department members in their search for the right course of action. Objectives and action plans provide procedures for reaching the law enforcement agency's destination.

The assessment phase evaluates arrival achievement, revises the department's vision, and suggests an appropriate future destination.

Intelligence analysts are primarily responsible for developing intelligence products, which coordinate information needs of internal and external customers.

Strategic and tactical products require decisive thinking across staff and line operations. Intelligence products that assist in meeting tactical, operational, and logistical requirements must be succinct and timely.

A formidable test requires converting data into a useful format, and convincing others of the significance and merits of ideas. Moreover, supplying intelligence to rightful customers is the eventual objective.

Analysts refine the intelligence product, and determine the needs of consumers through consultation and feedback.

Intelligence analysts brief commanders with reference to operational areas of criminal activity, and possible strategic and tactical outcomes.

Basic intelligence analyst responsibilities include collecting information or data from open and closed sources, followed by targeting known criminal organizations and criminals.

Raw data or information is not police intelligence. The collection process is the initial step, followed by critical analysis, conducted by a trained professional capable of critical thinking.

Problem solving is the third step, and the final step is proper dissemination of intelligence to those who have the need and right to acquire such data.

The intelligence analyst's position requires computer skills that enhance access to numerous national databases. Analysts collect and collate data, then validate information through successful queries of accessible databases.

Moreover, analysts confirm, identify conflicts, or refute contradictory information. Expert analysts employ information databases, think critically, organize reports, and present concise criminal information.

## Learning Objectives

- List the intelligence analyst responsibilities.
- List crime analyst responsibilities.
- Describe the management of intelligence operations.
- List key skill requirements for intelligence analysts.
- Identify the intelligence professional organization.
- Distinguish the connection between critical thinking and intelligence analysis.
- Connect the intelligence relationship among the ten coordinating strategies.

*Special Note:* Refer to the related Tables and Figures in the main text.

10

# Prologue - Questions

## Fill in the Blank
*Answers on page 123*

P-1. _____ analysts collect and analyze intelligence concerning enterprise criminals and their organizations.

P-2. _____ analysts collect and analyze street intelligence concerning serial crimes, i.e., burglary and robbery.

P-3. _____ analysts conduct psychological profiling and crime scene reconstructions.

P-4. _____ is a pioneer intelligence professional organization that supports intelligence analysts.

P-5. The concept of _____ applies to law enforcement intelligence analysis, strategic and tactical planning.

P-6. _____ is the master organizational strategy that guides the raw collection of criminal information in law enforcement agencies.


## Multiple Choice
*Answers on page 129*

1. Another name for Intelligence-Led Policing is intelligence _____ policing.

    a. Crime analysis
    b. Intelligence analysis
    c. Driven
    d. None of the above

2. Intelligence analysts are primarily responsible for the following choice(s):

   a. Intelligence products
   b. Crime analysis
   c. Operations analysis
   d. None of the above

3. Crime analyst responsibilities include which of the following choice(s):

   a. Collect and synthesize
   b. Supply information
   c. Street crime
   d. All of the above

4. Intelligence analyst responsibilities include which of the following choice(s):

   a. Strategic products
   b. Criminal organizations
   c. Enterprise crime
   d. All of the above

5. Criminal Investigative Analysis (CIA) includes which of the following choice(s):

   a. Serial crimes
   b. Crime scene reconstruction
   c. Modus operandi analysis
   d. All of the above

# CHAPTER 1
# INTRODUCTION

## Synopsis

The ILP management philosophy is an essential component of police organizational structure. The chief executive should define ILP as fundamental to the organizational climate. Senior leaders, middle managers, and supervisors require diverse ILP techniques to function effectively.

Intelligence analysis and accurate statistics assist in formulating critical thinking and vision for future planning. The ILP philosophical approach to policing reaches into every level of the law enforcement organization.

The United Kingdom's National Intelligence Model (NIM) advocates the concept of applying a business management model to law enforcement. The following questions require answers: (1) What is an accurate picture of the business? (2) What is actually happening on the ground or in the environment? (3) What is the nature and extent of the problem? (4) What are the trends? and (5) What is the main threat?

The NIM approach recommends that intelligence-led policing abide by the following objectives: (1) establish a task and coordination process, (2) develop core intelligence products to drive the operation, and (3) develop systems and protocols to facilitate the intelligence cycle. In addition, ensure successful training protocols for all levels of policing.

Intelligence analysts focus broadly on enterprise crime that has strategic and tactical applications. This form of analysis requires extensive planning and primarily deals with strategic long-range planning.

Intelligence analysts attack criminal organizations and their conspiracies. Intelligence analysis focuses on the correlation of certain elements of crime, and concentrates on names of individuals, and their connection to criminal organizations.

Strategic and tactical intelligence products are most effective when completed by professionals trained in analytic techniques. Intelligence analysis resides at the nucleus of the intelligence process.

Information does not become intelligence without analysis to derive meaning from data. Intelligence summaries and reports become products of analysis.

Crime analysis attempts to link such elements as suspect description and modus operandi connected to serial offenses. Crime analysis is more concerned with continuing street crimes, i.e., burglary, robbery, and auto theft. Crime mapping remains a critical component of the tactical planning process.

There are many intelligence analysis definitions and facets of meaning. The fundamentals include collection of raw data, analysis, and meaningful dissemination. The essential quality is excellent analysis of the information; otherwise, it is merely a collation of facts or raw data.

Critical thinking and logic represent foundations for the ILP management philosophy. Excellent logic and strategic planning leads to calculated goals, objectives, and tactical action plans. Proactive ILP intelligence gathering procedures provide support for intelligence and crime analysis strategies.

## Learning Objectives

- Define the role of intelligence analysis.
- Differentiate between ILP and intelligence analysis.
- Describe the Intelligence-Led Policing model.
- Describe the United Kingdom's National Intelligence model.
- Distinguish the elements of the Intelligence Cycle.
- List the elements of determining order of analysis.
- Identify the six-step process to intelligence dissemination.
- Identify open and covert sources of information.
- Identify threat assessment strategies.
- Identify the role of premonitories.

- Define aggressive analysis.
- Define intelligence estimate.
- Describe the assessment process.
- List the right to privacy legal protections.
- Identify the value of intelligence sharing.
- Identify the elements of the National Intelligence Sharing Plan.

*Special Note:* Refer to the related Tables and Figures in the main text.

## Chapter 1 - Questions

Fill in the Blank
*Answers on page 123*

1-1._____ addresses management coordination of the collection of intelligence at all levels of law enforcement organizations and serves as the driving component of the police business of intelligence.

1-2. The intelligence cycle is not a straight linear model, in practice it consists of many _____.

1-3. The collection process of the intelligence model addresses two general areas: _____ collection and _____ collection.

1-4. Federal regulations provide operators shall collect and maintain criminal intelligence concerning organizations and criminals based on _____ quantum of proof.

1-5. The two basic rules for intelligence dissemination are _____ and _____ basis.

1-6. Intelligence evaluation consists of two basic parts: _____ and _____.

1-7. The _____ has established a visualization of the National Criminal Intelligence Sharing Plan.

1-8. _____ is conducted prior to the commission of a crime and outside the general course of an investigation with long-range expectations.

1-9. _____ are short-range assessments that bridge the gap between strategic and tactical intelligence.

1-10. _____ quantifies the aggressiveness, and expansionist tendencies of a criminal enterprise to use force and intimidation.

## Multiple Choice
*Answers on page 129*

1. Intelligence analysis is directed at which of the following investigation(s):

    a. White collar
    b. Organized crime
    c. Enterprise crime
    d. All of the above

2. Intelligence-Led Policing can best be defined according to which of the following choice(s):

    a. Philosophy
    b. Management strategy
    c. Both a & b
    d. None of the above

3. Intelligence-Led Policing can best be described according to which of the following choice(s):

    a. Straight linear model
    b. Continuous cycles
    c. Philosophy
    d. None of the above

4. According to CFR, Part 23, the legal standard for the collection of intelligence information represents the following correct choice(s):

    a. Probable cause
    b. Reasonable suspicion
    c. Guilt beyond a reasonable doubt
    d. None of the above

5. Aggressive analysis attempts to quantify which of the following choice(s):

   a. Adventurous
   b. Expansiveness
   c. Intimation and violence
   d. All of the above

# Chapter 1 Focus Concepts

Table 1-1. Chapter Focus

| Intelligence-Led Policing | ILP Intelligence Concepts | ILP Intelligence Cycle |
|---|---|---|
| | ❖ ILP Intelligence Reorganization<br>❖ Intelligence Defined<br>❖ Intelligence Analysis<br>❖ Strategic Analysis<br>❖ Tactical Analysis<br>❖ Crime Analysis<br>❖ Criminal Investigative Analysis | ❖ Requirements & Collection<br>❖ Planning & Targeting<br>❖ Collection & Collation<br>❖ Processing & Analysis<br>❖ Evaluation & Production<br>❖ Dissemination<br>❖ Intelligence Products |
| | **ILP Sources of Information** | **ILP Information Sharing** |
| | ❖ Legal Requirements<br>❖ Open Sources<br>❖ Closed Sources<br>❖ Databases<br>❖ Media Reports<br>❖ Internet Searches<br>❖ Business Directories | ❖ Premonitories<br>❖ Strategic Assessment<br>❖ Intelligence Estimates<br>❖ Vulnerability Analysis<br>❖ Aggressive Analysis<br>❖ Intelligence Reporting<br>❖ Interdiction |

# CHAPTER 2
# ORGANIZATIONAL STRATEGIES

## Synopsis

Intelligence-Led Policing (ILP) philosophy suggests targeting specific organizational components to meet intelligence sharing requirements and the new organizational architecture. Successful reorganization eliminates non-functional organizational structure, and what remains is essential.

The ILP approach requires integration and consolidation of present strategies, offering police service uniformity. The ILP approach requires integration and consolidation of present strategies, offering police service uniformity. This approach recommends nomenclature standardization, and adopting ILP intelligence and related strategies.

Smaller police agencies may not require implementation of some formal and organizational components. Less urban agencies regularly rely on regional, state, federal, and other database support systems.

Leadership addresses intelligence procedures and operational priorities. Successful ILP implementation requires acceptance, cooperation, and commitment from all agency levels.

Open gateposts and organizational change becomes instrumental in achieving successful ILP execution. The starting point for developing the ILP management philosophy is an organizational definition.

ILP reflects an evolutionary strategic shift toward the development of a future-policing archetype, a holistic or blended paradigm.

The present multiplicity of overlapping police strategies requires organizational realignment to achieve intelligence-driven policing. Homeland security and accurate criminal intelligence planning serve the core of law enforcement operations.

The combined components of ILP offer a criminal information framework for community crime problems, and homeland security solutions. ILP + COPPS + CompStat = Intelligence Strategies and Tactics. Moreover, this formula offers focused policing that is target specific to particular crimes, and threats to homeland security.

The holistic approach, including the sum of its parts, equals more than the whole. The COP philosophy remains indispensable for all related strategies.

## Learning Objectives

- Describe Intelligence-Led Policing from a management perspective.
- List the elements of the COPPS equation.
- List the elements of COPPS, ILP, and CompStat equation.
- Describe the core elements of Community-oriented Policing.
- Describe the elements of Problem-oriented Policing.
- Describe the elements of CompStat.
- Identify elements of CompStat leadership strategies.
- Describe the assessment and effectiveness of leadership strategies.
- List the levels of police intelligence.
- Identify the elements of the new police intelligence architecture.
- Appraise the value of a synchronized holistic or blended paradigm.

*Special Note:* *Refer to the related Tables and Figures in the main text.*

# Chapter 2 - Questions

## Fill in the Blank
*Answers on page 123*

2-1. _____ reflects an evolutionary strategic shift toward the development of a future-policing archetype, a holistic or blended paradigm.

2-2. Most important, intelligence must be contingent on _____ analysis of data.

2-3. _____ is closely related in process to problem-oriented policing, and supplements CompStat leadership.

2-4. Positioning the _____ at the decentralized end of the spectrum, encourages positive momentum from the street, to highly centralized _____ operation.

2-5. _____ is the strategic arm of COP, and without the problem-solving component; the philosophy does not have the momentum to improve community quality of life issues, including level and fear of crime.

2-6. The application of _____, _____ and _____ responses enhanced crime prevention efforts and proved more effective than random patrol.

2-7. _____ is an essential ingredient of the CompStat process.

2-8. The _____ strategies are superior to the standard model, which offers little or no scientific evidence of effectiveness.

2-9. Focused policing acknowledges that a crime cannot occur devoid of three elements that form a crime triangle: (1) _____, (2) _____ and (3) _____.

2-10. _____ is a management concept in law enforcement that focuses on using intelligence products of decision-making at the strategic and tactical levels.

## Multiple Choice

*Answers on page 129*

1. According to your textbook, Intelligence-Led Policing requires which of the following choice(s):

    a. Integration
    b. Consolidation
    c. Standardization
    d. All of the above

2. The COP philosophy is primarily concerned with which of the following choice(s):

    a. Community empowerment
    b. Community feedback
    c. Citizen interaction
    d. All of the above

3. Problem-oriented policing is primarily concerned with which of the following choice(s):

    a. Quality of life issues
    b. Problem analysis
    c. SARA
    d. All of the above

4. CompStat is primarily concerned with which of the following choice(s):

    a. Leadership
    b. Statistics
    c. a & b
    d. None of the above

5. The new police architecture is primarily concerned with which of the following choice(s):

    a. Intelligence-Led Policing
    b. Intelligence driven policing
    c. a & b
    d. None of the above

# Chapter 2 Focus Concepts

Table 2-1. Chapter Focus

| | ILP Management Philosophy | ILP Policing Strategies |
|---|---|---|
| **Intelligence-Led Policing** | ❖ ILP Philosophy<br>❖ Policy Development<br>❖ Consolidation Strategies<br>❖ Reintegration & Organization<br>❖ Organization Strategies<br>❖ Blending Strategies<br>❖ ILP Defined | ❖ Community-oriented Policing<br>❖ Problem-oriented Policing<br>❖ SARA Planning Strategies<br>❖ CompStat Strategies<br>❖ Homeland Security<br>❖ Focused Policing<br>❖ Holistic Approach |
| | **ILP COP philosophy** | **ILP CompStat Leadership** |
| | ❖ COP Direction<br>❖ Citizen Interaction<br>❖ Attitudes & Values<br>❖ Police Cooperation<br>❖ Civic Cooperation<br>❖ Decentralized<br>❖ Citizen Feedback | ❖ Empowers Commanders<br>❖ POP & CompStat<br>❖ SARA Planning Process:<br>  ❖ Scanning<br>  ❖ Analysis<br>  ❖ Response<br>  ❖ Assessment |

# CHAPTER 3
# CRIME ANALYSIS STRATEGIES

## Synopsis

Intelligence-Led Policing (ILP) management operations and intelligence analysts should not exist disconnected and apart from crime analysis. There are four basic forms of crime analysis: (1) strategic, (2) tactical, (3) administrative, and (4) operations. The emphasis is on crime analysis critical thinking strategies.

Strategic analysis anticipates future crime trends and provides guidance to police commanders. The information helps law enforcement leaders deploy resources and predict future requirements.

Strategic analysis is: (1) the analysis of a crime group, (2) overall criminal activity, or situation, which (3) results in the production of a report or that group, activity or situation, and (4) includes recommendations for future actions.

Statistical reports may be included that reflect anticipated changes that indicate resource reallocations and updated acquisition requirements. The product of strategic analysis is often a strategic assessment, concerning a particular group threat.

Tactical crime analysis is the study of reported crime, calls for service, and related information. The analyst reviews, maps, and tabulates modus operandi, offender characteristics, spatial/or temporal factors, including victim or other characteristics. Once data is collected, crime mapping becomes an essential component of tactical crime analysis; spatial characteristics assist in linking criminal activity, relationships, and offender(s).

Administrative analysis involves the dissemination of findings, general data information, or non-specific crime research. The presentation is a brief summary that avoids in-depth research and statistical analysis. The information conference or media release should be brief, clear, and concise. In general, this information is not sensitive and appropriately presented in a public forum.

The audience may include local government, council members, and citizens. The objective is to inform diverse customers and audiences, remaining mindful of privacy requirements and respecting confidentiality. Appropriate security procedures value privacy, individual rights and avoid negative media releases.

Operations analysis provides information on police patrol practices. The analysis and information assists police leaders in planning patrol allocations and logistical support. Analytical information improves decision-making and the quality of police services, by examining workload responsibilities and personnel deployment.

Operations analysis: (1) is the analytical study of police delivery services, (2) provides commanders and police managers with a scientific basis for decisions, and (3) improves operations or resource deployment.

Operations analysis supports leaders who implement department planning, direction and control strategies. The related objectives and tasks sustain essential functions that support police operations.

Crime analysis data assists in the allocation of patrol deployment operations and determining logistical requirements. Target analysis defines: (1) target profile, (2) target selection, and (3) statistical analysis.

Target analysis profiles might identify criminal suspects who have a particularly rewarding modus operandi or propensity to commit certain kinds of criminal offenses. Target profile data might include: (1) time of attack, (2) type of attack, (3) location, and (4) target vulnerability.

Statistical analysis remains the foundation for tactical deployment of officers. Statistical geographic analysis defines areas that represent significant and recurring offenses. Geographic Information System(s) or crime mapping best serve this function when combined with statistical analysis.

ILP, COP, POP, and CompStat require crime analysis for successful crime prevention and intervention outcomes. Analysts are central to drawing inferences and conclusions.

They focus on the crime problem, judge the credibility of sources and deductions, and provide consequential recommendations, and effective courses of action. The final strategic and tactical actions are the responsibility of police commanders and leaders.

## Learning Objectives

- Define crime analysis.
- Define strategic intelligence.
- Define tactical intelligence.
- Define administrative analysis.
- Define operations analysis.
- Describe the tactical planning process.
- List the elements of profile analysis.
- Identify the elements of target selection.
- Define the function of statistics in police deployment and operations.
- Describe the function of geographical analysis in police operations.
- Identify the function of tactical crime linkage.
- Distinguish the following crime linkage terms: pattern, trend, series, spree, hotspot, hot product, and hot target.
- Describe Geographic Information Systems (GIS) applications to crime analysis.
- List the research applications for crime mapping.
- Identify the elements of crime mapping tactical analysis.

*Special Note:* *Refer to the related Tables and Figures in the main text.*

## Chapter 3 - Questions

### Fill in the Blank
*Answers on page 124*

3-1. There are four basic forms of crime analysis: (1) _____, (2) _____, (3) _____ and (4) _____.

3-2. _____ is the systematic study of crime and disorder problems, as well as other police-related issues, including socio-demographic, spatial, and temporal factors, to assist police in criminal apprehensions, crime and disorder reduction, crime prevention, and evaluation.

3-3. Criminal analysis is the field of study, and three areas of sub-disciplines are related: (1) _____, (2) _____, and (3) _____.

3-4. _____ is: (1) the analysis of a crime group, (2) overall criminal activity, or situation, which (3) results in the production of a report of that group, activity, or situation and (4) includes recommendations for future actions.

3-5. _____ is the study of reported crime, calls for service and related information. The analyst reviews, maps and tabulates modus operandi, offender characteristics, spatial or temporal factors, including victim or other characteristics.

3-6. _____ involves the dissemination of findings, general data information, or non-specific crime research. The presentation is a brief summary that avoids in-depth research and statistical analysis.

3-7. _____ provides information on police patrol practices.

3-8. Target analysis defines: (1) _____, (2) _____, and (3) _____.

3-9. _____ analysis, occasionally defined as victim profiling, identifies persons, structures, vehicles, or other entities, as potential crime targets.

3-10. _____ analysis remains the foundation for the tactical deployment of officers.

3-11. A _____ is an arrangement or order discernable in any crime-related phenomena.

3-12. A _____ is a specific type of pattern that assumes a general direction or tendency.

3-13. A _____ characterizes a high frequency of criminal activity, to the extent that it appears almost continuous.

3-14. A _____ run of similar crimes connected to the same individual(s), disconnected in time.

3-15. A hot _____ is a specific location or small area where an unusually high level of criminal activity occurs, that is committed by one or more offenders.

3-16. A hot _____ is an individual associated with an unusual amount of criminal activity, either as an offender or a victim.

3-17. A hot _____ is a specific type of property that is the target in similar or different types of crime.

3-18. A hot _____ refers to a particular type of frequently victimized target, not included in the previous definitions of hot spots (small areas), hot dots (persons), or hot products (goods).

3-19. There are two primary reasons for repeat victimization; one, known as the _____ explanation, relates to the role of repeat offenders; the other, known as the _____ explanation, relates to the vulnerability or attractiveness of certain victims.

3-20. Routine activity theory specifies basic elements of a crime: (1) _____, (2) _____, and (3) _____.

3-21. Victimization occurs primarily due to exposure to crime opportunity, and target opportunity. Therefore, the police should _____, _____, and _____ offenses.

3-22. GIS _____ is an integral component of the crime analysis process and intelligence cycle, which leads to accurate criminal intelligence.

## Multiple Choice

*Answers on page 129*

1. Crime analysis is the systematic study of crime. Which of the following choice(s) describes its mission:

    a. Socio-demographic
    b. Spatial
    c. Temporal
    d. All of the above

2. Strategic intelligence is defined by which of the following choice(s):

    a. Long-term
    b. Future recommendations
    c. Strategic assessment
    d. All of the above

3. Tactical analysis is best described by which of the following choice(s):

    a. Study of reported crime
    b. Modus operandi analysis
    c. Offender characteristics
    d. None of the above

4. Operations analysis is best described by which of the following choice(s):

    a. Patrol allocation
    b. Logistical allocation
    c. Objective driven
    d. All of the above

5. Which item on the list is not one of the four basic forms of crime analysis:

   a. Strategic
   b. Tactical
   c. Administrative
   d. Investigative

# Chapter 3 Focus Concepts

Table 3-1. Focus Points (Crime Analysis Concepts)

| | Critical Thinking Concepts | Crime Analysis Concepts |
|---|---|---|
| **Intelligence-Led Policing** | ❖ Favorable Mind Habits<br>❖ Drawing Inferences<br>❖ Noting Observations<br>❖ Focusing on the Problem<br>❖ Analyzing Positions<br>❖ Judging Credibility<br>❖ Judging Decisions | ❖ Crime Analysis<br>❖ Analytical Processes<br>❖ Strategic Analysis<br>❖ Strategic Planning<br>❖ Tactical Analysis<br>❖ Administrative Analysis<br>❖ Operations Analysis<br>❖ Trend Correlations |
| | **Tactical Strategies** | **Geographic Information Systems** |
| | ❖ Tactical Planning<br>❖ Tactical Analysis<br>❖ Target Selection<br>❖ Statistical Analysis<br>❖ Geographical Analysis<br>❖ Tactical Crime Linkage<br>❖ Patrol Deployment | ❖ Crime Mapping<br>❖ Visual Grammar<br>❖ Mapping Symbols<br>❖ Mapping Layers<br>❖ Geocoding<br>❖ Hot Spots<br>❖ Clusters<br>❖ Circles |

# Chapter 4
# CompStat Integration

## Synopsis

*Intelligence-Led Policing: Leadership, Strategies, and Tactics* bridges the gap between strategic leadership, intelligence, and crime analysis operations. ILP represents an intelligence management system that coordinates criminal information sharing. ILP and COP philosophy concepts support effective police practices.

Problem-oriented Policing (POP) and SARA provide the long to mid-range strategic planning model. Intelligence analysis supports long-term strategies, and threat assessment preparation.

The CompStat leadership model offers short-term planning for street and emergency tactical operations. CompStat strategies encourage crime-fighting tactics that utilize: (1) crime analysis, (2) leadership and emphasize, (3) tactical strategies.

The integration and coordination of ILP, POP, and CompStat are essential to the successful execution of crime prevention, and intervention efforts.

The synchronization of policing strategies, avoids competing and counter-productive outcomes. Therefore, the policing paradigm equation represents the following formula: ILP + COP + POP + CompStat = Consolidated Intelligence and Coordinated Decision-Making.

A unified command, occupying the same location and centralized control, is the essence of ILP management philosophy. In addition, the central office would supervise decentralized intelligence/crime analysts attached to police operation and investigative functions.

The consolidation of intelligence and crime analysis is a basic organizational requirement for achieving information sharing, and integrated analysis. The next logical step requires the synchronization of POP and CompStat policing strategies.

The philosophy of community-oriented policing is firmly in the fabric of American policing. However, the planning process incorporates POP and SARA strategies to realize COP philosophy goals and objectives.

These problem-solving strategies focus on crime generators and hot spots, which distress communities. CompStat enhances the COP and POP models, and when properly coordinated, the tripod can improve police effectiveness in large police agencies.

## Learning Objectives

- Distinguish the role of POP and SARA in the planning process.
- Describe the SARA planning model.
- List the SARA planning stages.
- Identify the elements of CompStat.
- Identify the steps for integrating CompStat leadership requirements.
- Identify the role of intelligence requirements for POP and CompStat.
- Identify the need for crime pattern information.
- Describe the value of integrated police strategies.

*Special Note:* *Refer to the related Tables and Figures in the main text.*

## Chapter 4 - Questions

### Fill in the Blank
*Answers on page 124*

4-1. _____ coined the term and expressed a general theory for the POP theory, and SARA planning strategies.

4-2. The police department successfully experimented with the SARA Planning model: _____, _____, _____, and _____.

4-3. The POP and SARA planning strategies are essential components of _____.

4-4. _____ patrol officers, anti-crime officers, and detectives communicate with each other.

4-5. Analyzing crime trends and patterns is important because: If you can _____ it, you can _____ it.

4-6. Effective tactics require planning: _____ to plan is _____ to fail.

4-7. CompStat staff meetings emphasize _____, _____, and _____ results.

4-8. The CompStat paradigm places accountability with _____, rather than headquarters executives and street officers.

4-9. The POP strategies are _____, not _____.

4-10. Regardless of the size of the policing agency, coordination with _____, _____, _____, and _____ sharing resources are of paramount importance.

## Multiple Choice

*Answers on page 129*

1. Problem-oriented Policing (POP) can provide planning support for which of the following choice(s):

    a. CompStat
    b. Long-term Planning
    c. Operations analysis
    d. All of the above

2. POP is most closely associated with which of the following choice(s):

    a. Long-range to mid-range planning
    b. Mid-range to short-range planning
    c. Emergency operations planning
    d. None of the above

3. The SARA planning model is most closely associated with following except:

    a. Scanning
    b. Analysis
    c. Rapid deployment
    d. Assessment

4. CompStat's main point of administrative coordination is which of the following choice(s):

    a. HQ command element
    b. Patrol officer
    c. Staff strategy meetings
    d. COP operations

5. Crime pattern information is best connected to which of the following choice(s):

    a. Repeat offenders
    b. Single offense operations
    c. Both a & b
    d. None of the above

# Chapter 4 Focus Concepts

Table 4-1. Focus and Concepts

| | ILP Intelligence Integration | ILP SARA Planning Strategies |
|---|---|---|
| Intelligence-Led Policing | ❖ Community-oriented Policing<br>❖ Intelligence-led Policing<br>❖ Intelligence Analysis<br>❖ Intelligence Cycle<br>❖ Crime Analysis<br>❖ Problem-solving Policing<br>❖ CompStat Tactics | ❖ Define the Problem<br>❖ Scanning<br>❖ Analysis<br>❖ Response<br>❖ Focus on the Causes of Crime(s)<br>❖ Focus on Systematic Inquiry<br>❖ Assessment |
| | **ILP Problem-Solving Policing** | **ILP CompStat Leadership** |
| | ❖ Problem-solving Policing<br>❖ Proactive Responses<br>❖ Develop Partnerships<br>❖ Focus on Underlying Causes<br>❖ Group Incidents as a Problem<br>❖ React to Underlying Problems<br>❖ Develop Tailor-made Responses | ❖ Crime Fighting Strategies<br>❖ Accurate and Timely Intelligence<br>❖ Teamwork<br>❖ Staff Coordination<br>❖ Rapid Deployment<br>❖ Effective Tactics<br>❖ Relentless Follow-up and Assessment |

38

# Part II
## Strategic Leadership

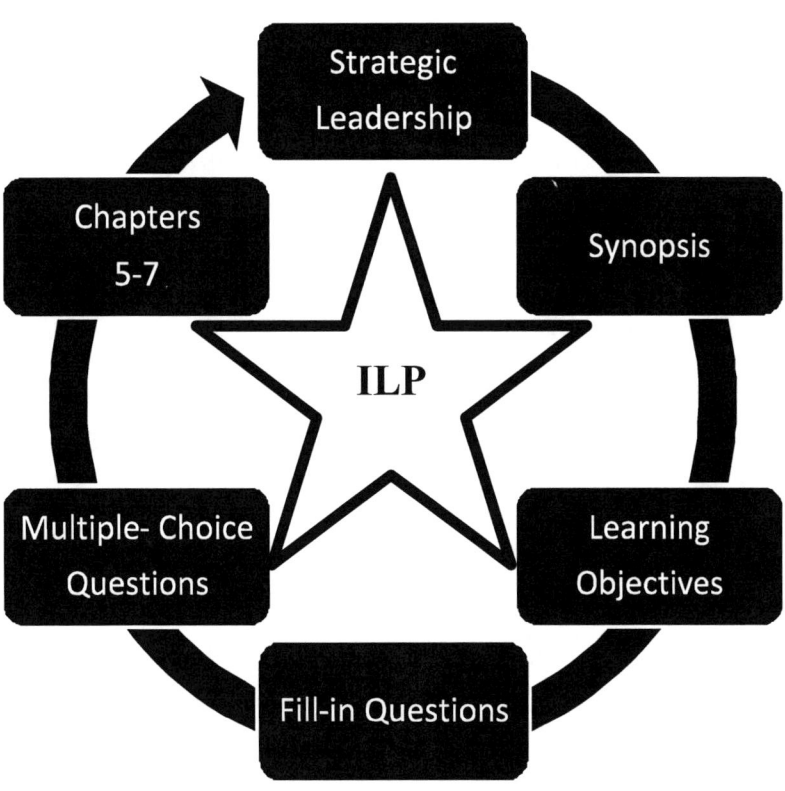

# Chapter 5
## Strategic Leadership and Communication

## Synopsis

The "Johari Window" encourages the expansion of shared intelligence and achieving accurate feedback, but requires personal risks for leaders. The ILP management/leadership style requires candid leaders who establish trust and mutual respect.

Excellent leadership suggests information exchanges, rather than one-way dialogues, not involving feedback.

Feedback provides information concerning how organization members feel about and perceive leadership behaviors. Open leaders who are willing to disclose, encourage opportunities to understand how others feel about their leadership.

Stone-faced leaders deny followers opportunities to disclose feelings because of poor approachability, the façade, and the absence of leader feedback.

The Johari Window offers leaders the possibility of expanding personal power. Feedback is the reaction of officers and civilians (feelings and perceptions), thereby informing leaders about how his/her behaviors affect them.

Leaders equipped with crucial feedback are in the best position, to be effective decision-makers. Candid leaders amplify communication and feedback, enhancing follower information and support.

The lack of feedback is a statement in itself; it is a silent announcement about the police leader's effectiveness. Poor reciprocal communication isolates and places the leader outside the informal communication loop.

Police leaders, who hide behind their façade, or remain silent and do not take risks, fail to communicate and remain isolated.

Open police leaders who ask for feedback and disclose information about self, position themselves to influence others.

The willingness to self-disclose affects multiple relationships in police organizations. Disclosure and openness works in a variety of organizations, group situations, or with individuals.

Communication techniques do not require disclosing the intimate details of one's life.

The goal is to obtain information not known to self, but known to others. The opportunity to gain information from the blind spot, and unknown portions of the four Johari quadrants, proves essential to successful decision-making.

Sharing information from the hidden area (sometimes referred to as the façade) of the leader, provides greater understanding for subordinates to follow and share feedback.

Leadership self-disclosure encourages rapport and trust relationships with individual officers, civilians, informal groups and the police organization.

Peering into the Johari Window allows police leaders to expose the façade or the hidden area (the issues others do not know about the leader).

The purpose is to gain sufficient knowledge about the blind spot and unknown (the issues police leaders do not know about).

Thus, shrinking the windowpanes or quadrants around the blind spot ultimately offers insight into the unknown area and related issues. Insight provides opportunities to communicate, seize initiatives, and problem solve with appropriate strategic and tactical remedies.

The open space is the key to personal power, the quadrant, or windowpane where leaders have opportunities to be authentic and open.

Openness allows for the exchange of what one knows about self and what others know. This form of personal leadership interaction and risk taking invites feedback for effective decision-making.

# Learning Objectives

- Distinguish the relationship between leadership and vision.
- List the elements of a mission statement for Intelligence-Led Policing.
- Describe an overview of the Johari Window Model.
- Define the following Johari Window terms: hidden area, public area, blind area, and unknown.
- Describe the feedback concept.
- Identify the Johari Window Model's relationship to police strategic leadership.
- Identify the value of the Johari Window in the intelligence sharing process.
- Identify the Johari Window function concerning field operations applications.
- Describe the value of the NYPD's Real Time Crime Center (RTCC).

***Special Note:*** *Refer to the related Tables and Figures in the main text.*

## Chapter 5 - Questions

### Fill in the Blank
*Answers on page 125*

5-1. Leaders may not choose the right course of action in the decision-making process, not because of existing _____, but from the _____.

5-2. Unwillingness to _____ intelligence is a major obstacle to receiving appropriate and timely feedback.

5-3. Two psychologists, Joseph Luft and Harry Ingham, conceived the "Window Model" as a means of giving and receiving information _____.

5-4. The ILP management/leadership style requires candid leaders who establish _____ and mutual respect.

5-5. _____ provides information concerning how organization members feel about and perceive leadership behaviors.

5-6. The lack of feedback is a statement in itself; it is a silent announcement about the leader's _____.

5-7. The opportunity to gain information from the _____, and _____ portions of the four Johari quadrants, proves essential to successful decision-making.

5-8. Peering into the Johari Window allows police leaders to expose the façade of the _____ (the issues others do not know about he leader).

5-9. Shrinking the windowpanes or quadrants around the _____ spot ultimately offers insight into the _____ area and related issues.

5-10. The _____ space is the key to personal power, the quadrant, or windowpane where leaders have opportunities to be authentic.

5-11. Communication may involve _____ or _____ cues and learner perceptions.

5-12. The centralization and coordination of criminal information and computer technology offer improved _____ feedback communication.

5-13. The New York City Police Department (NYPD) _____ Crime Center demonstrates the classic example of computer technology and improved feedback communication.

5-14. The RTCC includes three key elements: the _____ warehouse, the _____ capabilities, and the "data wall," part of the nerve center of the RTCC.

5-15. The ILP and strategic planning process, along with informed leadership, _____ future strategic requirements.

5-16. Timely leadership preparedness is important; however, _____ is even more imperative.

5-17. Successful leaders access the public area, and use it to launch admittance to the _____ and _____ areas.

**Multiple Choice**
*Answers on page 129*

1. The Johari Window Model is primarily concerned with which of the following choice(s):

    a. Social problems
    b. Crime analysis
    c. Feedback
    d. None of the above

2. The main problem expressed by the Johari Window Model concerning feedback concerns which of the following choice(s):

    a. Façade
    b. Poor image
    c. Two-way communication
    d. All of the above

3. The Johari Window offers police leaders the possibility of expanding which of the following choice(s):

    a. Formal power
    b. Bureaucratic power
    c. Position power
    d. Personal power

4. The hidden area refers to which of the following choice(s):

    a. Façade
    b. Blind spot
    c. Unknown
    d. None of the above

5. Shrinking the windowpanes or quadrants around the blind spot ultimately offers some insight into which of the following choice(s):

   a. Façade
   b. Unknown
   c. Blind spot
   d. b. and c.

# Chapter 5 Focus Concepts

Table 5-1. Focus Points

| | Vision and Direction | Leadership and Goals |
|---|---|---|
| Intelligence-Led Policing | <ul><li>Envision the future</li><li>Past is starting point</li><li>Apply analytical skills</li><li>Modify and share feedback</li><li>Define vision statement</li><li>Define ILP</li><li>Lead up front</li></ul> | <ul><li>Change, grow, and innovate</li><li>Inspire a shared vision</li><li>Enable others to act</li><li>Role model, so others may follow</li><li>Plan small wins that build commitment</li><li>Encourage the heart</li><li>Celebrate team accomplishments</li></ul> |
| | **Johari Window Strategies** | **Decision-Making Opportunities** |
| | <ul><li>Leaders are candid</li><li>Willingness to disclose self</li><li>Avoid façade or hidden area</li><li>Personal power in public area</li><li>Gain access to blind area</li><li>Gain access to unknown area</li><li>Obtain behavior feedback</li></ul> | <ul><li>Johari Window analysis</li><li>Leadership applications</li><li>Training applications</li><li>Internal applications</li><li>External applications</li><li>Share intelligence</li><li>Expand communication base</li></ul> |

# Chapter 6
# Leadership Planning

## Synopsis

Planning bridges the gap between where the agency is presently, and where officials want police ILP services to go. The planning process helps identify and select successful methods to achieve positive goals and objectives. Defining how the police agency will reach their desired destination involves an excellent analytical planning process.

Planning involves determining target needs and a basic definition of the problem. The following criteria are essential to the planning process: (1) suspense date for accomplishment, (2) location, (3) officer allocations, (4) those held responsible for the mission, and (5) mission operational requirements.

Planning and ILP management have mutual goals and objectives; therefore, both are not mutually exclusive.

Strategic planning cannot exist in a vacuum, without ILP management of criminal information and mutual feedback. ILP intelligence analysis and feedback permits strategic planning to function effectively. Moreover, quality coordination with tactical planners avoids counterproductive outcomes in high profile strategic cases.

Large metropolitan law enforcement agencies require seven points of planning linkage: (1) police decision makers and central strategic planning, (2) intelligence-led policing, (3) intelligence analysis, (4) crime analysis, (5) community-oriented policing, (6) problem-oriented policing and (7) CompStat operations. Police leaders serve as central points of coordination and key decision makers.

The essence of the traditional synoptic planning model is future decision-making. Centralized planning forms the foundation for critical thinking, and strategic intelligence analysis. ILP and intelligence analysis can support: (1) problem-oriented policing and SARA planning, (2)

CompStat and operations analysis, (3) emergency operations planning, (4) incident action planning, and (5) evaluation. The synoptic planning model forms a natural conduit for the consolidation of these mutual planning foundations.

EOP planning focuses on developing an operational document, which incorporates a written response plan for emergency operations. The threat assessment process identifies vulnerable targets and potential terrorists or other emergency responses.

Strategic plans list interagency responsibilities, the chain of command, and logistical support. Basic planning concepts have application to many communities. However, individual community adaptations are the individualizations of the basic model.

Occasionally, some agencies may refer to the EOP as a comprehensive emergency management plan. The coordination of police, fire, and emergency services receive special emphasis; however, military coordination is a component of the planning process. The emphasis is on agency liaison coordination, front-end planning, and logistics.

The terrorist incident action and tactical response plan is an essential element of EOP operations. The plan incorporates a model approach and unified command similar to military operations. The basic organization includes: (1) planning, (2) management and administration, (3) personnel and operations, and (4) logistics.

The incident action plan is a standard course of action, relevant to a real-time possible scenario. Written tactical plans address serious incidents; less significant incidents do not require written documentation.

IAP applies to a specific operational time, and in some instances, the incident planning process may unfold informally as the changing emergency scenario continues.

An impromptu briefing may take place in the field that includes a brief outline of protocols, and mission objectives. Extended missions may require formal briefings on a prearranged schedule.

Evaluation is necessary to redirect the leadership process, and help reorient the planning process. It answers three crucial questions: (1) Has the agency arrived? (2) Where is the agency now? (3) Where does the agency go from here? It provides the map for developing strategic goals and objectives; furthermore, it provides plans for directing officers to new specific tasks.

The evaluator gleans information that guides the leadership in a decision-making process. The process reduces uncertainty and assists police officers in emergency responses. Lessons learned in the after-action briefing, form the basis for revising the planning process, and changing goals, objectives, and procedures.

## Learning Objectives

- Define the role of police planning in the ILP management process.
- List the goals of effective planning.
- Define strategic planning.
- Define the term "operational intelligence planning."
- Describe the synchronization of the planning process.
- Describe the need for centralized planning.
- List the elements of the strategic planning process.
- List the six points of planning linkage.
- Identify the role of Emergency Operations Planning (EOP).
- Define the elements of an Incident Action Plan (IAP).
- Identify the role of timing in the planning process.
- Describe the role of fusion centers.
- List the elements of the intelligence cycle planning.
- Describe the intelligence targeting process.
- Define the vital intelligence elements of the Target Centric Approach.
- List the elements of the crime triangle.
- Describe the target selection information and selection process.

***Special Note:*** *Refer to the related Tables and Figures in the main text.*

## Chapter 6 - Questions

**Fill in the Blank**
*Answers on page 125*

6-1. _____planning is global in nature, and offers a quality research point of view.

6-2. _____ primarily identifies the strengths, weaknesses, opportunities, and threat analysis of selected targets.

6-3. Strategic planning includes advanced _____, and large scope problems.

6-4. The _____ of the planning process, promotes opportunities for successful tactical outcomes.

6-5. _____ bridges the gap between where the agency is presently, and where officials want police ILP services to go.

6-6. Planning and ILP management have mutual _____ and _____; therefore, both are not mutually exclusive.

6-7. _____ planning focuses on developing an operational document, which incorporates a written response plan for emergency operations.

6-8. Occasionally, some agencies may refer to the EOP as a comprehensive _____ management plan.

6-9. The _____ incident action and _____ response plan is an essential element of EOP operations.

6-10. The _____ action plan is a standard course of action, relevant to a real-time possible scenario.

6-11. An _____ briefing may take place in the field and includes a brief outline of protocols, and mission objectives.

6-12. Planning support incorporates _____ planning procedures for personnel requirements, and logistical supplies.

6-13. _____ is essential; intelligence requirements that support the tactical mode necessitate fluency.

6-14. _____ analytical support has current intelligence and real-time requirements that parallel the need for crime analysis.

6-15. Police _____ centers may offset fast responses through planned coordination and liaison activities.

6-16. Incoming data requires a _____ synthesis when supporting short-time or in-progress police tactical operations.

6-17. The intelligence cycle reinforces the _____, _____, and _____ process.

6-18. _____ criminals and their organizations provide direction for police responses.

6-19. A _____ approach or objective-oriented intelligence process provides a model for targeting.

6-20. A crime cannot occur without three elements that form the crime triangle: _____, _____, and _____.

6-21. Familiarity with a neighborhood reinforces criminal patterns, a process often referred to as _____ mapping or _____ imaging.

6-22. Offenders plan potential crimes and make decisions based on _____ information.

6-23. Opportunity, reward, and fear of arrest determine the difference between _____ and _____ crime hot spots.

## Multiple Choice

*Answers on page 129*

1. Effective planning can accomplish which of the following choice(s):

    a. Problem analysis
    b. Clarify goals
    c. Coordination
    d. Provide direction
    e. All of the above

2. Strategic planning includes which of the following choice(s):

    a. Statistical analysis
    b. Short-term targets
    c. Tactical responses
    d. None of the above

3. Identify the following overlapping processes for strategic intelligence planning. Which answer represents best of the following choice(s)?

    a. CompStat
    b. POP
    c. Tactical planning
    d. None of the above

4. The essence of the synoptic planning process is best represented in which of the following choice(s):

    a. Short-term
    b. Future
    c. Tactical
    d. None of the above

5. Emergency Operations Planning (EOP) primarily focuses on which of the following choice(s):

    a. Strategic document
    b. Tactical document
    c. Operational document
    d. None of the above

# Chapter 6 Focus Concepts

Table 6-1. Chapter focus

| | Planning Synchronization | Centralized |
|---|---|---|
| **Intelligence-Led Policing** | ❖ Police Decision-makers<br>❖ Intelligence Coordination<br>❖ Intelligence Analysis<br>❖ Crime Analysis<br>❖ Community-oriented Policing<br>❖ Problem-oriented Policing<br>❖ Compstat Operations | ❖ Ilp Management<br>❖ Defining Planning<br>❖ Planning Articulation<br>❖ Staff Coordination<br>❖ Synoptic Planning<br>❖ Emergency Operations Planning<br>❖ Incident Action Planning |
| | **Johari Window Strategies** | **Decision-Making Opportunities** |
| | ❖ Define the Problem<br>❖ Suspense Date<br>❖ Location<br>❖ Officer Allocations<br>❖ Mission Responsibilities<br>❖ Operational Requirements<br>❖ Staff Coordination | ❖ Target-centered Planning<br>❖ Crime Triangle<br>❖ Fusion Centers<br>❖ Current Intelligence<br>❖ Short-term Intelligence<br>❖ Immediate Intelligence<br>❖ Real Time Intelligence |

# CHAPTER 7
# ANALYTICAL PRODUCTS

## Synopsis

Intelligence-Led Policing (ILP) is an analytical management process that produces reliable reports for intelligence purposes concerning crime trends, crimes, and community security threats.

Skillful intelligence analysis, expertise, and training produce superior intelligence finished products. Analytical reporting serves as the foundation for the ILP philosophy and management system.

Intelligence products illustrate many types of analytical frames of reference. Finished products vary according to the needs of customers and criminal case situations.

The basic products include: (1) written reports, (2) verbal presentations, and (3) background papers or estimates. Intelligence products unfold at three main levels of intelligence analysis: (1) strategic, (2) tactical, and (3) operational.

Strategic products are broadly based focused papers or estimates, which involve intelligence research. The strategic product is generally expansive; details may include other graphic related support documents.

Projections envision future events and include conceptual models capable of prediction, or estimating present and future outcomes. Useful product applications include global enterprise crime, terrorism, and other complicated conspiracy crimes. For example, systems analysis products may involve international drug cartel structures, systems functionality, systems maintenance, and financial profits.

Tactical target products may include profiles, biographies, and confirmation of criminal networks. Finished intelligence products for street gangs may include: (1) organizational structure, (2) association analysis,

(3) criminal activities, and (4) geographical factors affecting law enforcement operations.

Tactical analytical products may prove essential in burglary rings, drug operations, street gangs and other on-going tactical or local operations.

Operational intelligence reporting is primarily internal to law enforcement organizational structure and logistical necessities.

The planning process centers on strategic and tactical requirements for law enforcement operations, which may include personnel, supplies and communications, etc.

The depth of analysis and length of reporting strategies vary according to the situation, topic, or criminal activity. The same products may fit both strategic and tactical strategies, and include analytical graphic support. In addition, shared intelligence, that informs, may have multiple applications at various levels of criminal activities.

## Learning Objectives

- Describe the need for intelligence products.
- Describe the elements of a written report.
- Describe the elements of a verbal report.
- List the three main levels of intelligence analysis products.
- List the elements of tactical reporting.
- Identify the elements of operational reporting.
- List the elements of effective dissemination requirements.
- List the seven finished intelligence products.
- Describe the need for superior field intelligence reporting.
- Describe the purpose of the Quarterly Trend Report.
- Describe the purpose of the Strategic Threat Assessment Report.
- Identify the elements of the Warning Report.
- Identify the elements of the Crime Bulletin Report.
- Describe the need for review and assessment of intelligence reports in the main text.

*Special Note: Refer to the related Tables and Figures in the main text.*

# Chapter 7 - Questions

## Fill in the Blank
*Answers on page 126*

7-1. Intelligence-led Policing (ILP) is an analytical management process that produces reliable reports for intelligence purposes concerning _____, _____ and community _____.

7-2. Analytical _____ serves as the foundation for the ILP philosophy and management system.

7-3. _____ products are broadly-based focused papers or estimates, which involve intelligence research.

7-4. _____ envision future events and include conceptual models capable of prediction or estimating present and future outcomes.

7-5. Tactical target products may include _____, _____, and _____ of criminal networks.

7-6. _____ intelligence reporting is primarily internal to law enforcement organizational structure and logistical necessities.

7-7. Finished analytical intelligence products include: (1) _____, (2) _____, (3) _____, (4) _____, (5) _____, (6) _____, and (7) _____.

7-8. The primary purpose of the _____ briefing is to provide a "situation orientation" for initial planning.

7-9. The _____ briefing's purpose is to secure a decision from the Chief of Police or senior leaders.

7-10. A _____ briefing is a final review of a planned action to ensure participants are confident in their understanding of the objectives.

7-11. A _____ report's most common rationale is to disseminate important time-critical intelligence without regard to a specific schedule.

7-12. The primary means of collecting information from the field remains _____ reporting.

7-13. The _____ format delivers concise information that allows straightforward formatting, collection and collation.

7-14. The purpose of the _____ is to describe significant changes of the operating environment.

7-15. _____ analysis identifies the intent and capabilities of criminal group activities.

7-16. The _____ report generally flows from the threat or vulnerability assessment.

7-17. Crime _____ contain brief analytical statements and often warn about a specific criminal or particular criminal activity.

7-18. _____ identify lessons learned about specific events and police actions.

7-19. _____, _____, and _____ intelligence products are the foundation for effective police leadership.

7-20. _____ intelligence addresses daily events, apprises consumers of new developments, and provides consequence warnings.

## Multiple Choice
*Answers on page 129*

1. Intelligence analytical products assist police leaders concerning which of these area(s):

    a. Decision-making
    b. Strategic applications
    c. Tactical applications
    d. All of the above

2. Intelligence analytical products have which of the following goal(s):

    a. Accurate view of the crime problem
    b. Forecasting
    c. Intervention and Prevention
    d. All of the above

3. Strategic research products focus on which of the following choice(s):

    a. Narrow approach
    b. Broad approach
    c. Tactical approach
    d. None of the above

4. _____ conveys specific intelligence operations details to a select audience in a concise format, which of the following is the best choice(s):

    a. Written report
    b. Briefing
    c. QTR Report
    d. None of the above

5. Current intelligence is best described by which of the following choice(s):

    a. In-depth
    b. Consequence warning
    c. Sound alarm
    d. None of the above

# Chapter 7 Focus Concepts

Table 7-1. Chapter Focus

| | Introduction: Intelligence Products | Intelligence Product Levels |
|---|---|---|
| **Intelligence-Led Policing** | ❖ Definition: Intelligence Product<br>❖ Developing Criminal Information<br>❖ Integrated Perspective<br>❖ Strategic Products<br>❖ Tactical Products<br>❖ Operational Products<br>❖ Assessment Products | ❖ Written Report Products<br>❖ Verbal Presentations<br>❖ Background Products<br>❖ Estimate Products<br>❖ Near-term Products<br>❖ Projection Products<br>❖ Prediction Products |
| | **Product Standards** | **Types of Analytical Products** |
| | ❖ Basic IALEIA Standards<br>❖ Procedures<br>❖ Central Collection Point<br>❖ Rapid Retrieval<br>❖ Record Systems<br>❖ Identified Data Sources<br>❖ Dissemination Requirements | ❖ Field Information Report<br>❖ Briefing<br>❖ Spot Report<br>❖ Quarterly Trend Report<br>❖ Threat Assessment Report<br>❖ After-action Report<br>❖ Graphic Analytical Products |

# PART III
# TACTICAL APPLICATIONS

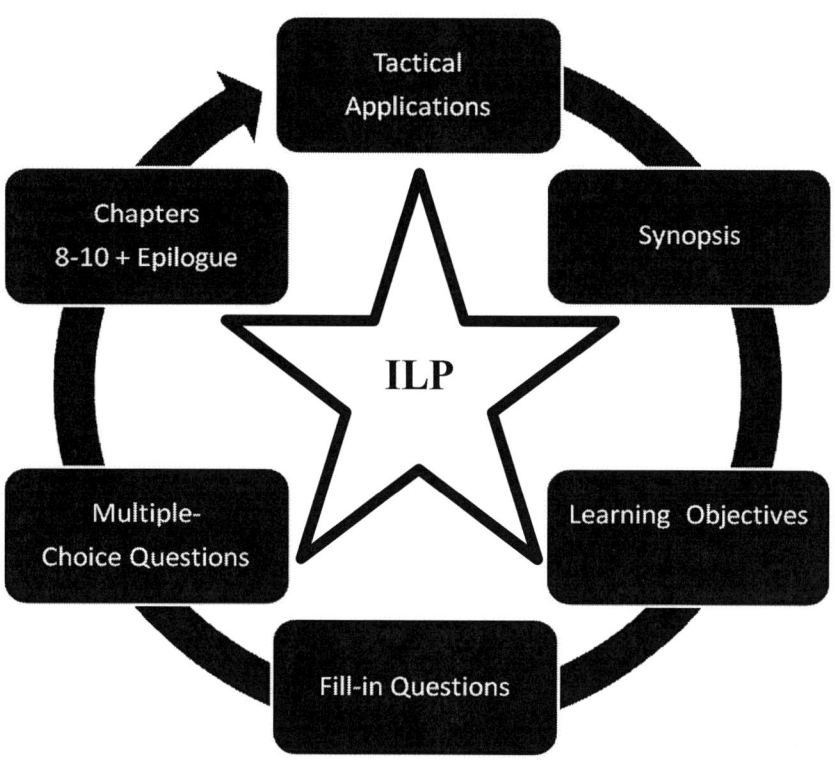

# Chapter 8
# Analytical Models and Charting

## Synopsis

Intelligence-Led Policing (ILP) is an analytical management process that produces reliable reports for intelligence purposes concerning crime trends, crimes, and community security threats. Skillful intelligence analysis, expertise, and training produce superior intelligence finished products.

Analytical reporting serves as the foundation for the ILP philosophy and management system.

Intelligence products illustrate many types of analytical frames of reference. Finished products vary according to the needs of customers and criminal case situations.

The basic products include: (1) written reports, (2) verbal presentations, and (3) background papers or estimates.

Intelligence products unfold at three main levels of intelligence analysis: (1) strategic, (2) tactical, and (3) operational.

Strategic products are broadly-based focused papers or estimates, which involve intelligence research. The strategic product is generally expansive; details may include other graphic related support documents.

Projections envision future events and include conceptual models capable of prediction or estimating present and future outcomes. Useful product applications include: (1) global enterprise crime, (2) terrorism, and (3) other complicated conspiracy crimes. For example, systems analysis products may involve international drug cartel structures, systems functionality, systems maintenance, and financial profits.

Tactical target products may include: (1) profiles, (2) biographies, and (3) confirmation of criminal networks. Finished intelligence products for street gangs may include: (1) organizational structure, (2) association analysis, (3) criminal activities, and (4) geographical factors affecting law enforcement operations.

Tactical analytical products may prove essential in burglary rings, drug operations, street gangs, and other on-going tactical or local operations.

Operational intelligence reporting is primarily internal to law enforcement organizational structure and logistical necessities. The planning process centers on strategic and tactical requirements for law enforcement operations, which may include personnel, supplies and communications, etc.

Police operational intelligence is closer to near term operations, involving considerable planning and support of specific operations. Final products clarify support operations and deployment information for officers.

Police senior leaders, middle managers and supervisors need timely, actionable intelligence, for the criminal targeting process. Analysts prefer to present intelligence products, and not become involved in the leadership decision-making process.

Analysts produce intelligence products: (1) reports, (2) models, and (3) analytical charting, that support crime fighting endeavors and community solutions.

Police leaders make decisions that lead to positive prevention and intervention outcomes.

The visual presentation identifies an analytical overview of the facts, recommendations, and tactical applications. These analytical graphics clearly render the complex relationships in enterprise crime and their criminal networks for investigators.

A visual charting diagram illustrates suspects, patrons, locations, and demonstrates criminal relationships.

Analytical charting and analysis offer strategic and tactical insight opportunities. Graphic and visual snapshots provide valuable insight into criminal enterprise strategies.

Reviewing written reports may obscure important concepts and facts that could successfully conclude the investigation. Charting strategies address salient facts in an efficient manner.

The foundation for intelligence analysis is surveillance, informants and field interviews. The completed "intelligence product" may include brief biographical sketches and charting analysis, that illustrate the hierarchy leadership's strengths and vulnerabilities.

Excellent intelligence analysis pieces together information that link the actions of criminals to specific intelligence products, for field investigators.

The following intelligence products are applicable to ILP operations. The list is not inclusive; new strategies are constantly emerging.

The main analytical charting strategies include: (1) event flow analysis, (2) association analysis, (3) commodity flow analysis, and (4) VIA investigative analysis. In addition, key graphic analysis include: (5), network analysis, (6) risk analysis, (7) financial analysis, (8) telephone record analysis and (9) other graphic visual formats.

Accurate intelligence analysis, reporting, models, and charting enterprise criminal operations, focus spotlights on criminals. Coordination and sharing of criminal intelligence counters enterprise crime threats, and can make a positive difference concerning prevention, intervention, and prosecution.

## Learning Objectives

- Describe the need for analytical intelligence reporting.
- Describe the need for analytical model products.
- Describe the need for analytical charting products.

- List the elements of descriptive analytical intelligence reporting.
- List the elements of explanatory analytical intelligence reporting.
- List the elements of predictive analytical intelligence reporting.
- List the elements of pattern analysis.
- Describe the use of Analyst's Notebook computer systems.
- Identify the various basic analytical charting products.
- Identify the need for review and assessment of intelligence reports in the main text.

*Special Note:* Refer to the related Tables and Figures in the main text.

## Chapter 8 - Questions

### Fill in the Blank
*Answers on page 126*

8-1. Analytical support documents provide police and civilian analysts massive details in a _____ portrait of crime.

8-2. Police commanders require analysts' critical thinking analytical _____ and _____ products, for successful decision-making.

8-3. Intelligence analysts produce graphs, charts, and reports that support complex investigations of a _____ nature.

8-4. Basic analytical models and charting strategies assist investigator understanding of complex criminal _____ and their human relationships.

8-5. Analytical reports for police decision-makers are concise, clearly written, and preferable under _____ pages.

8-6. _____ are directly associated with targeting criminal behavior and support the investigative process.

8-7. _____ and analytical _____ documents support investigative teams as they approach complex conspiracy crimes.

8-8. A _____ is a symbolic representation of an actual system; it is a substitute for the real system.

8-9. _____ developed the Crime Prevention Through Environmental Design Model.

8-10. There are four basic CPTED elements of defensible space: (1) _____, (2) _____, (3) _____ and (4) _____.

8-11. The CPTED concept term _____ refers to the ability and desire of legitimate users to claim the area.

8-12. The second CPTED concept, _____, refers to designing an area that allows legitimate users to observe.

8-13. The CPTED model concept, _____, suggests that the placement of the community in a larger context is important.

8-14. The LAPD built a buffer zone among gangs with Operation Cul-de-Sac (OCDS), and applied the Newman _____ model.

8-15. Using Analyst's _____, analysts can uncover and interpret the relationships and patterns hidden within their data, displaying them in intuitive charts.

8-16. _____ flow analysis generally precedes association and commodity flow analysis early in the investigation.

8-17. _____ analysis remains the cornerstone of enterprise intelligence; it can describe the criminal organization and its relative strength.

8-18. Association Analysis and HMINT set the foundation for _____ the human intelligence factor, i.e., human support systems.

8-19. _____ Flow Analysis identifies the distribution network, and money traced to key individuals.

## Multiple Choice

*Answers on page 129*

1. A _____ is a symbolic representation of an actual system; it is a substitute for the real system. Which of the following would be the best choice(s):

    a. Chart
    b. Model
    c. Cycle
    d. None of the above

2. Pattern analysis describes which of the following choice(s):

    a. Modus operandi
    b. Atcherly's system
    c. Both a & b
    d. None of the above

3. The Enterprise Model is best described by which of the following choice(s):

    a. External model
    b. Internal model
    c. Both of the above
    d. None of the above

4. The Analysts' Notebook software is best described by which of the following choice(s):

    a. Tracing patterns
    b. Charting analysis
    c. Both a and c
    d. None of the above

5. Newman's Designing-out Model is best described by which of the following choice(s):

    a. Pattern analysis
    b. Reinforcing engineering concepts
    c. Both a and b
    d. None of the above

# Chapter 8 Focus Concepts

Table 8-1. Chapter Focus

| | ILP Analytical Formats | ILP Analytical Standards |
|---|---|---|
| **Intelligence-Led Policing** | ❖ Descriptive Analytical Reporting<br>❖ Explanatory Analytical Reporting<br>❖ Visualization<br>❖ Future Forecasting<br>❖ Reporting Brevity<br>❖ Supporting Research<br>❖ Decision-making | ❖ Planning Standard<br>❖ Direction Standard<br>❖ Collection Standard<br>❖ Collation Standard<br>❖ Legal Standard<br>❖ Evaluation Standard<br>❖ Follow-up Standard |
| | **ILP Analytical Standards** | **ILP Visual Reporting** |
| | ❖ Analytical Accuracy<br>❖ Computerized Standard<br>❖ Content Standard<br>❖ Outcomes Standard<br>❖ Report Standard<br>❖ Product Format Standard<br>❖ Dissemination Standard | ❖ Analytical Models<br>❖ Analytical Charting<br>❖ Event Flow Analysis<br>❖ Association Analysis<br>❖ Commodity Flow Analysis<br>❖ Telephone Analysis<br>❖ Via Charting |

# CHAPTER 9
# INVESTIGATIVE STRATEGIES

## Synopsis

Intelligence-Led Policing (ILP) targets career criminals and repeat offenders. ILP targets career felony offenders and their criminal organizations on the belief that they are responsible for significant amounts of serious crime.

The key basic ILP tools for investigating complex conspiracy crimes include: (1) human intelligence or HUMINT, primarily informants, undercover operations and surveillance procedures, (2) communications intelligence or COMINT, primarily electronic surveillance, i.e., wiretapping.

The synopsis addresses: (1) analytic strategies for conspiracy crimes, (2) informants, (3) undercover operations, (4) physical surveillance tactics, and (5) electronic surveillance. The topics emphasize the ILP connection to conspiracy crimes and related requirements.

Enterprise crime is an expansive concept; the definition continues to grow and operates outside the boundaries of traditional and organized crime. For example, enterprise crime offenses include environmental crime, and trafficking in body parts.

Targeting career felony offenders and their organizations can be a successful strategy for reducing repeat offenses and the level of crime. Opportunities for enterprise crime are abundant, including new global venues created for international criminals.

Undercover operations include high risks and rewards. Deep cover operations are expensive; however, when successful, the ultimate source of real-time criminal information. Undercover operations require excellent planning, management, and supervision.

Intelligence sharing is a two-way endeavor, including field intelligence feedback from officers and intelligence analysis flowing to the undercover or deep cover operatives. Officers in the field cannot operate in a void or make cases without direction and adequate intelligence.

Informants are primary investigative tools; they operate in the criminal environment, have a trusted status, and intercept criminal information. The best informant is "under the gun," facing huge criminal charges and penalties, the second best is the revenge type. Excellent informant handlers control informants, place restrictions on informant behavior, and assist with possible betrayals.

Physical surveillance is the straightforward approach to assessing criminal patterns and interaction. Physical surveillance, informants, and pen-registers of telephone calls serve as the foundation for the ultimate goal of wiretapping.

Wiretapping and other forms of electronic surveillance are last resort investigative tools. Constitutional law regulates and dominates the application of electronic interceptions.

In summary, the basic keys for investigating enterprise crime are human intelligence (HUMINT) and communication intelligence (COMINT). Human intelligence includes, but is not limited to informants, undercover operations, and physical surveillance. Electronic communications include, but are not limited to wiretapping, and a host of other electronic tools.

## Learning Objectives

- List the key basic tools for investigating complex conspiracy crimes.
- Define HUMINT.
- Define COMINT.
- Define the enterprise concept from an enforcement perspective.
- List the types of crimes that fall under the enterprise crime theory.
- Define the elements of the crime of conspiracy.
- Describe the elements of the Informant Management Program.
- Describe the elements of successful law enforcement undercover operations.

- List the elements of deep cover planning.
- Identify the elements of undercover operations planning.
- Define the two basic types of physical surveillance.
- Describe the strategies of the A-B-C surveillance system.
- List the basic provisions of electronic surveillance.
- Define the term pen-register.
- Define telephone analysis.
- Define financial analysis.
- Describe the need for review and assessment of intelligence reports in the main text.

*Special Note:* Refer to the related Tables and Figures in the main text.

# Chapter 9 - Questions

### Fill in the Blank
*Answers on page 127*

9-1. _____ crime represents a wide-ranging concept, encompassing an expansive range of economic, white collar, fraud, and organized crimes.

9-2. Criminal offenses are committed because both _____ and _____ markets meet the laws of supply and demand.

9-3. The _____ and networking of a nation's economy has numerous systemic implications for enterprise criminals.

9-4. A criminal _____ consists of two or more persons who engage in a criminal agreement.

9-5. _____ remain central to ILP management criminal information requirements.

9-6. The _____ and _____ of any effective law enforcement agency enterprise control program remain a well-controlled informant program.

9-7. Informants are assigned _____; investigators avoid using their names in reports.

9-8. Informant status is a _____ priority because it is a life/death issue for informants and undercover officers.

9-9. _____ sworn operatives perform best when there is intensive strategic planning, tactical and accurate intelligence support.

9-10. The objective of a _____ officer is to dismantle the criminal enterprise leadership structure.

9-11. Teams that _____ together prior to operations _____ together.

9-12. There may be a prearranged designated _____ or pick-up location for undercover _____ and less important communications.

9-13. Deep cover officers must never feel that they are a _____ operation without support.

9-14. The principles of physical surveillance include two basic types: (1) _____ surveillance, and (2) _____ surveillance.

9-15. This kind of _____ surveillance works best in moderate traffic.

9-16. The application of _____ analysis, _____ analysis, and _____ analysis assists in identifying key members of criminal enterprise.

9-17. The _____ forms the foundation for ex parte authorization; technology intercepts telephone calls made or received and call duration.

9-18. The former KGB deliberately released hard-core criminals from their prisons, concluding the infamous _____ criminals or thieves with a code of honor.

9-19. The swindle involved a _____ with a vanishing point; transferring gasoline on paper from one bogus company to another delayed the opportunity for auditors and investigators to discover the violations.

9-20. Numerous global enterprise organizations have a flexible, _____ leadership structure.

## Multiple Choice
*Answers on page 129*

1. Enterprise crime is most closely associated with which of the following choice(s):

    a. Street crime
    b. Crime analysis
    c. Conspiracy crimes
    d. None of the above

2. Russian Organized Crime (ROC) structure as described by its members can be identified by which of the following choice(s):

    a. Mob
    b. Highly structured
    c. Brigades
    d. None of the above

3. ROC structure can best be described by which of the following choice(s):

    a. Highly structured
    b. Loosely structured
    c. Traditional structure
    d. None of the above

4. ROC criminal activities involved gas fraud, and can be best described by the following choice(s):

    a. Extortion
    b. Daisy chain
    c. Vory
    d. None of the above

5. Tracking the money is essential to solving enterprise conspiracy cases, analysis finds the money-trail, which is the best choice(s):

    a. Event flow analysis
    b. Association analysis
    c. Commodity flow analysis
    d. None of the above

# Chapter 9 Focus Concepts

Table 9-1. Chapter Focus

| | Enterprise Crime | Investigative Tools |
|---|---|---|
| **Intelligence-Led Policing** | ❖ Global Concept<br>❖ White Collar Crime<br>❖ Organized Crime<br>❖ Drug Trafficking<br>❖ Cyber Crimes<br>❖ Human Trafficking<br>❖ Selling Human Body Parts | ❖ Human Intelligence<br>❖ Communications Intelligence<br>❖ Undercover Operations<br>❖ Physical Surveillance<br>❖ Informants<br>❖ Electronic Surveillance<br>❖ Intelligence Sharing |
| | **Informant Management** | **Undercover Operations** |
| | ❖ Central Ilp Management<br>❖ Centralized Database<br>❖ Control and Corroboration<br>❖ Classifying Informants<br>❖ Supervising Informants<br>❖ Collecting and Reporting<br>❖ Criminal Information | ❖ Personnel Selection<br>❖ Planning<br>❖ Team Training<br>❖ Team Deployment<br>❖ Carrying out Operations<br>❖ Operation Termination<br>❖ Reintegration |

# CHAPTER 10
## TACTICAL LEADERSHIP: TRAINING

## Synopsis

Antiterrorism procedures are important leadership requirements for preventing terrorist operations. The proactive intelligence role requires denying terrorists intelligence on police operations and intelligence gathering methods.

Areas of antiterrorism prevention include: (1) operations security, (2) personnel security, (3) physical security, and (4) crisis management planning. The goal of antiterrorism operations is to deny criminals and terrorists police information.

Once an incident occurs, police operations move to the reactive stage for performing crisis management and counterterrorism tactics. Excellent ILP and proactive prevention seeks to avoid tactical scenarios.

Excellent threat/risk management, crime prevention, and physical security programs assist in avoiding crisis management scenarios.

Dynamic planning articulates responsibilities and remedial responses for public safety agencies. Effective leadership, realistic training, and case study simulations, enhance tactical responses.

The themes address techniques of antiterrorism, counterintelligence procedures, combating and detecting potential terrorist acts.

Antiterrorism is the first phase of the program; defensive measures include basic internal police and external target vulnerabilities. Threat assessment includes: (1) crime prevention and (2) physical security mandates.

Threat assessment leads to successful crime prevention, physical security goals, and objectives. Effective threat analysis requires countering disinformation and deception, while determining trend lines and exact intelligence themes.

In the second phase, counterterrorism takes the offense and provides mechanisms to respond to terrorist initiatives. This phase implements sound planning procedures after a terrorist incident.

The second phase response is timely and insures public safety. Special reaction or SWAT teams require integrated training programs, which are inter-jurisdictional in nature.

Law enforcement agencies plan and coordinate terrorism countermeasures. Counterterrorism planning requires constant revisions and real world applications.

Excellent planning mandates learning simulations, including active exercise scenarios, which require interagency coordination. The emphasis is on strategic and tactical flexibility to law enforcement operations.

Superior intelligence analysis requires in-depth strategic and tactical planning. The planning cycle focuses on terrorists, and plans for the possibility of a direct assault on law enforcement operations.

Planning avoids casualties, and the possibility of reduced law enforcement services, during a terrorist incident.

ILP and planning remain essentials to analyzing the terrorist threat; successful leadership applies the threat analysis equation.

Excellent analysis requires constant review and assessment of security, crime prevention plans, and developing strategies addressing crime prevention, operations security, physical security, and personnel security.

Superior proactive strategies include excellent planning, awareness, and educational programs.

Tactical planning must be flexible, and includes commanders who adjust plans when conditions change. Planning can be effective in responding to emergency incidents, combating terrorism and the emergency planning process.

The combination of accurate and timely intelligence, rapid deployment, effective tactics and relentless follow-up, provides a foundation for terrorism, homeland security and unfolding criminal patterns.

Finally, leadership implies being in control of self, others, and the tactical mission. Sergeants create a positive social climate by setting attainable objectives and clearly defined standards. Leadership by example and frontline presence remains the foremost requirement of influencing officers. High-quality leadership demonstrates the mature perspective of self-control and leads from the frontlines.

## Learning Objectives

- Define antiterrorism responsibilities.
- List the three antiterrorism planning strategies.
- Define counterterrorism responsibilities.
- List the elements of counterterrorism planning.
- Describe the role of the intelligence analyst in the terrorism assignment.
- Define the intelligence biographical sketch.
- Define the terrorist group profile.
- List the five interconnected processes that are essential to understanding terrorism.
- Identify the need for police operations security.
- Define INFOSEC.
- Define police physical security.
- Define police personal security.
- Define the term threat analysis.
- List the elements of the threat analysis formula.
- Describe the purpose of the crime prevention survey.
- List the first two components in the first phase of the antiterrorism program.
- Identify the essential elements of crisis management planning.
- Describe the basic field planning objectives.
- Define the term goal.
- Define the term objective.
- Explain the role of tactical leadership.

- Identify the four basic styles of NIJ police supervision.
- Identify the best NIJ leadership style for frontline tactical missions.
- Describe the need for review and assessment of intelligence reports in the main text.

*Special Note:* Refer to the related Tables and Figures in the main text.

## Chapter 10 - Questions

### Fill in the Blank
*Answers on page 127*

10-1. Areas of antiterrorism prevention include (1) _____, (2) _____, (3) _____, and (4) _____.

10-2. Counterterrorism techniques include the response to an _____ specific terrorist act.

10-3. _____ sketches and photographs support the analytical techniques.

10-4. The _____ sketch identifies data particular to the suspect, for example, aliases, addresses, vehicles, and business associations.

10-5. Terrorist groups are easier to profile than _____.

10-6. Taking basic security precautions and developing antiterrorism _____ and counterterrorism _____ programs can reduce critical target vulnerability.

10-7. _____ is an important law enforcement issue: traditionally, enterprise or terrorist crime is the main concern.

10-8. _____ denies potential information to individuals who are "not authorized" or "do not need to know" confidential information.

10-9. _____ analysis is a tool to measure and analyze intelligence information.

10-10. _____ surveys focus on the social fabric and human interaction.

10-11. _____ focuses on technology, lights, locks, and access control.

10-12. _____ management planning remains the foundation for tactical leadership.

10-13. Four models of police supervision identified by the National Institute of Justice (NIJ): (1) _____, (2) _____, (3) _____ and (4) _____.

10-14. Clearly, _____ supervisors offer minimal field contact, support, and opportunities to influence police officers.

10-15. _____ leaders seek field encounters, teachable moments, and support police officers.

## Multiple Choice
*Answers on page 129*

1. Antiterrorism areas of responsibility are best described by which of the following choice(s):

   a. Special reaction teams
   b. Intelligence summaries
   c. Physical security
   d. None of the above

2. Counterterrorism planning is best described by which of the following choice(s):

   a. Physical security
   b. Personnel security
   c. State of readiness
   d. None of the above

3. Antiterrorism planning is best described by which of the following choice(s):

   a. Reactive
   b. Proactive
   c. Fixed
   d. None of the above

4. Which of the following choice(s) best describes counterterrorism?

   a. Reactive
   b. Proactive
   c. Preventative
   d. None of the above

5. There are four models of leadership identified by the National Institute of Justice (NIJ); which of the following choice(s) would have the most influence with their officers:

   a. Traditional
   b. Active
   c. Innovative
   d. Supportive

## Chapter 10 Focus Concepts

Table 10-1. Chapter Focus

| | ILP Police Strategies | ILP Intelligence Analyst Roles |
|---|---|---|
| Intelligence-Led Policing | ❖ Antiterrorism Strategies<br>❖ Counterterrorism Strategies<br>❖ Intelligence Summary<br>❖ Operations Planning<br>❖ Threat Analysis<br>❖ Swat Teams<br>❖ Lessons Learned | ❖ Intelligence Analysis<br>❖ Analytical Charting<br>❖ Biographical Sketches<br>❖ Terrorist Profiling<br>❖ Terrorist Group Profile<br>❖ Model Building<br>❖ Asymmetrical Warfare Intelligence |
| | **ILP Antiterrorism Strategies** | **ILP Counterterrorism Leadership** |
| | ❖ Proactive Planning<br>❖ Police Operations Security<br>❖ Personnel Security<br>❖ Physical Security<br>❖ Crisis Management<br>❖ Opsec Security Measures<br>❖ Crime/physical Security Prevention Surveys | ❖ Tactical Training<br>❖ Learning Simulations<br>❖ Tactical Leadership<br>❖ Frontline Leadership<br>❖ Frontline Behaviors<br>❖ Frontline Feedback<br>❖ Field Planning |

# Epilogue
# Concluding Focus Points

## Synopsis

A clear sense of vision enables the police to understand the importance of diverse strategies, which allow police agencies to "arrive" and achieve improved crime control, prevention and homeland security. The formidable goal becomes possible with proactive ILP strategic and tactical intelligence planning, supported by excellent police strategic leadership.

ILP and successful policing strategies determine much of what transpires. The synchronization of strategies is preferable to competing strategies. Moreover, blending strategies requires cooperation and assimilation into the ILP management philosophy.

(1) The consolidation and synthesis of Community-Oriented Policing (COP) + Problem-Oriented Policing (POP) + SARA planning model = COPPS.

(2) The new intelligence-led policing approach would include: ILP + COPPS + CompStat + Quality Leadership = Police Excellence.

(3) The strategic formula is: ILP Organization + Intelligence Analysis (IA) + Crime Analysis (CA) + Collection (C) + Storage (S) + Computer Analysis (CA) + Dissemination (D) = Criminal Intelligence (CI).

(4) Finally, the new intelligence-led policing grand strategy would include: ILP + COPPS + CompStat + Quality Leadership = Police Excellence.

Integration and synchronization requires superior planning to achieve the goal of effective administration. Leaders must seize opportunities to implement effective strategies. The following four equations support the "grand theory" of ILP and much of what transpires.

## Learning Objectives

- Identify the ten basic articulated strategies of the text.
- Describe the central planning model.
- Identify the element of Intelligence-Led Policing.
- Describe the basic components of Intelligence-Led Policing synchronization.
- List the four formulas that support the "Grand Theory" of ILP.
- Describe the need for review and assessment of intelligence reports in the main text.

*Special Note:* Refer to the related Tables and Figures in the main text.

## Epilogue - Questions

### Fill in the Blank
*Answers on page 128*

E-1. O.W. Wilson, Father of Modern Policing, commented: "Next to total war the greatest threat to society is _____."

E-2. Commanders understand that they are ultimately responsible for _____ decisions.

E-3. _____ represents the new organizational nomenclature and management philosophy.

E-4. _____, analysis, and timely dissemination to those who need the information define the Intelligence Cycle core.

E-5. Social change impediments may emerge from the: (1) _____, (2) _____, and (3) _____.

E-6. Human interpersonal communication remains the primary facilitator in the _____ and _____ of any innovation.

E-7. Regardless of agency size, someone needs to address _____ and planning issues.

E-8. The Intelligence Cycle is the ____, ____, and ____ of criminal information, which benefits law enforcement agencies, and the nation.

E-9. ____ analysis forms the foundation for the analysis of street crime and CompStat operations.

E-10. Intelligence analysis is strategic and ____; crime analysis is tactical and ____.

E-11. Crime prevention ____ provide core information concerning criminal behavior for police patrol and tactical applications.

E-12. Similar to problem-oriented policing, ____ planning approaches crime problems by considering underlying factors that characterize each type of offense.

E-13. Intelligence reporting is the ____ of ILP management.

E-14. The National Security Agency operates a global spy system, entitled ____.

E-15. According to the Federal Bureau of Investigation, ____ is a sophisticated computerized-based system (protocol decoder) designed to capture e-mail or electronic communications.

## Multiple Choice
*Answers on page 129*

1. The crime triangle can best be described by which of the following choice(s):

    a. Offender
    b. Victim
    c. Crime Scene or location
    d. All of the above

2. The global spy program that can capture and analyze telephone calls, faxes, and telecommunication can best be described by which of the following choice(s):

    a. DCS-1000
    b. ECHELON
    c. ISP
    d. None of the above

3. The Federal Bureau of Investigation has a protocol decoder to capture e-mail or electronic communications; which of the following choice(s) describes the system:

    a. DCS-1000
    b. ECHELON
    c. C-code breaker
    d. None of the above

# Epilogue Focus Concepts

Table E-1. Epilogue (28 Realignment Concepts)

| | ILP Strategic Leadership | ILP Intelligence Cycle |
|---|---|---|
| **Intelligence-Led Policing** | ❖ "Thin Blue" Line<br>❖ the "Grand Strategy"<br>❖ Influence Process<br>❖ Decision-making<br>❖ Strategic Planning<br>❖ Proactive Operations<br>❖ Strike Criminals & Organizations | ❖ Requirements & Collection<br>❖ Planning & Targeting<br>❖ Collection & Collation<br>❖ Processing & Analyzing<br>❖ Evaluation and Production<br>❖ Dissemination<br>❖ Influence Decision-makers |
| | **ILP Policing Strategies** | **Eliminate Barriers** |
| | ❖ Intelligence-led Policing<br>❖ Community-oriented Policing<br>❖ Problem-oriented Policing<br>❖ Sara Planning Process<br>❖ Strategic Planning<br>❖ Compstat<br>❖ Strategies & Tactics | ❖ Excellent Communication<br>❖ Johari Window & Feedback<br>❖ Intelligence Driven Analysis<br>❖ Intelligence Sharing Process<br>❖ Regional & State Coordination<br>❖ Federal Coordination<br>❖ Realignment Sharing Process |

# Conclusion

The first step in the active learning process is to read assigned chapters and related materials; the second step is to read the summaries in this learning guide; the third step is to look up the learning objectives; the fourth step is to follow-up on the practice exercises; and the fifth and last step is to take the practice tests.

For the best learning results, avoid looking up the answers while taking the tests. Find out why you missed the correct choices, after taking practice tests. Move to Part V to take the practice tests, after reviewing the main text's Chapters, Tables, Figures and practice exercises in Part IV.

# PART IV
## INSTRUCTIONAL CONTENT

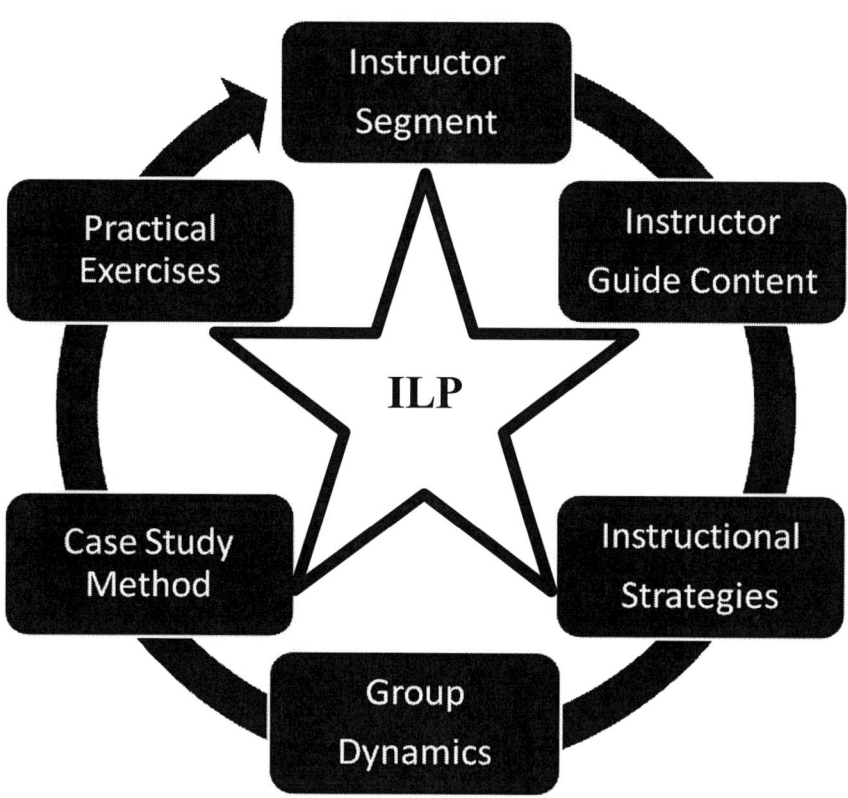

# Instructor Segment

The Instructor Segment's purpose is to assist police and academic instructors with direction for preparing classroom-learning experiences. The general organization described in the preceding pages involves learning progressions of increasing complexity and difficulty. The instructional strategies utilize diverse methods to reach varied learning styles. The methods incorporate an active learning approach that applies critical thinking, problem-solving, decision-making opportunities, and theoretical application skills.

The instructor's section and preliminary course outline assist in the instructional and learning process. Instructors are encouraged to modify, delete, and expand the course outline. Instructors vary their teaching methods; however, individual planning assures effectiveness and arriving on time.

## Instructor Guide Content

Intelligence-Led Policing: Leadership, Strategies, and Tactics: primary objective is to bridge the gap between strategic leadership, intelligence, and crime analysis operations. Intelligence-Led Policing is the management system and philosophy that coordinates sharing criminal information.

**The book and guide are for police leaders and officers seeking promotion to command positions.**

The secondary audience would include students of criminal justice, criminal analysis, and intelligence and Homeland Security programs. These new programs are emerging on the certificate, Associate Degree, Bachelor of Science and Master's Degree level.

Intelligence-Led Policing: Leadership, Strategies, and Tactics plus the Instructional Strategies and Promotion Guide are directly from the leadership, and intelligence management perspective.

The objective of the book is to inform police leaders concerning the value of Intelligence-Led Policing (ILP), criminal intelligence and crime analysis as effective leadership decision-making protocols.

(a) This intelligence-led policing book and guide are about applying the crime fighting strategies and tactics as a leadership and management style. In addition, the content prepares the reader for present or future leadership and command responsibilities.

(b) The Intelligence-led policing and instructional guide serve as a reader friendly learning instrument, rather than a dissertation or bureaucratic presentation style. This project seeks to integrate the concepts in favor of application and retention of the descriptive information.

(c) Outstanding features: The text has short focus points, learning objectives and practice tests. The key concepts serve as excellent illustrations for supporting the themes. The case studies offer readers opportunities to understand the material from the application point of view. This text and guide seek to be an easy read on the fundamentals that makes difficult material uncomplicated to the reader.

(d) Learning is an interactive process, which means that reading is only one part of the equation. The retention rate soars when the learner takes an active role in the learning process. The supplemental guide adds an additional active component.

(e) The technology revolution and related software have changed the leadership equation. Innovative intelligence strategies and rapid real-time intelligence sharing can literally make the difference between life and death decision-making.

## Instruction/Curriculum

Teaching Intelligence-Led Policing (ILP) from active learning and critical thinking perspectives is essential to learner understanding. The application and integration of theory and practice enhances learning and retention. The text addresses diverse learning styles. Case studies, Power-

Point, and programmed supplements support opportunities to apply newly acquired knowledge.

The ability to implement relevant concepts remains basic to independent thinking. Higher learning progressions improve with quality instructional strategies. Critical thinking serves as the foundation for analytical applications.

## Instructional Strategies

Collaborative group instruction encourages the ability to work with others and share information. Learners enjoy self-paced opportunities to master ILP concepts. Instructors encourage the free exchange of ideas, and exploration of possible solutions.

Small group offers opportunities for discussion, learner feedback, and reciprocal from peers and the instructor. Critical thinking skills unfold as learners become involved in their own instruction, cooperative interaction, and active learning. At times, the autonomous activities take on a life of their own, as students move in creative and imaginative thinking.

## Case Study Method Applications

Analyzing case studies creates opportunities for critical and creative thinking. This instructional application of ILP strategies provides opportunities for stimulating free discussion, and "brainstorming applications of the academic content." The cases can be real or hypothetical and describe a scenario that provides for learners to apply their knowledge. The practical case study exercises listed below are a starting point for critical thinking applications.

## Practical Exercise: Prologue

The Hometown police department is interested in the process of hiring an Intelligence-Led Policing manager. As the intelligence officer and commanding officer of the unit, your assignment is to write the job description and supervise the hiring process.

Refer to the PROLOGUE, Table P-1: Staff Requirements and Figure P-1: NCIP'S Recommendations for Guidance. Include your own observations in the written assignment.

## Practical Exercise: Chapter 1

Recently, your police assignment changed from the Homicide unit to the Intelligence Unit. This is a temporary assignment until a civilian can replace you. You have the responsibility of writing a strategic intelligence estimate on two motorcycle gangs currently operating in your community: Pagans and Warlocks.

These gangs have notorious reputations for activities that include: (1) illegal drugs, (2) prostitution, assault, and murder. The most important consideration is their influence in drug trafficking.

Write a strategic intelligence estimate, approximately ten pages in length. Refer to the Jamaican Posse case study in chapter one for an illustration. Address the following intelligence concepts: (1) threat assessment process, (2) aggressive analysis, (3) and vulnerability analysis.

Apply the Intelligence Cycle to open sources and refer to Chapter 1, Table 1: Threat Analysis Strategies, Figure 1-3: Intelligence Six Step Process to Dissemination, and Figure 1-2: Intelligence Cycle.

## Practical Exercise: Chapter 2

The Chief of Police, Commander of Staff and Administration Bureau, and Intelligence Commander are in the process of developing the new architecture for Intelligence-Led Policing. The Central Planning Committee has requested that you provide an organizational chart that blends and synchronizes: (1) Community-oriented Policing (COP), Problem-oriented Policing (POP), CompStat operations, and ILP.

The goal is to integrate independent operations under the ILP architecture. The new organizational chart would reflect the centralization of overlapping functions.

Submit this one-page chart based upon the content in Chapter 2, Table 2-2: Problem-oriented Policing, Table 2-3: CompStat Leadership Strategies, Table 2-5: Levels of Intelligence, Table 2-6: Blended Holistic Paradigm, and Figure 2-2: New Architecture.

## Practical Exercise: Chapter 3

You serve as the crime analyst for the new ILP Unit. The Commander requests a tactical analysis report of the recent series of community bank robberies. The goal is to develop tactical planning strategies for the purpose of prevention and intervention. The report length should be approximately five pages.

Refer to Chapter 3, and examine the key concepts: (1) target profile analysis, (2) statistical analysis, (3) and geographical analysis. Read the Case Study Example, The Analyst Briefing, for an example of the application of basic crime analysis concepts. In addition, refer to Table 3-2: Modus Operandi Criteria, Table 3-2a: Trademark Behaviors, and Figure 3-1: Generalizations Applications to the Use of Maps.

## Practical Exercise: Chapter 4

A series of commercial burglaries have recently plagued Hometown City. The burglars attack small and large retail stores in the downtown areas. They also include neighborhood stores, restaurants, and gas stations. More recently, the pattern has changed to a local national banking service.

As the commander of the research unit, you are responsible for the POP planning and CompStat coordination. Describe how Intelligence-Led Policing plays a significant part of centralization of intelligence and crime analysis to support this robbery problem.

Refer to Chapter 4, Figure 4-1: ILP Integration Strategies, Figure 4-2: ILP Communication and Feedback, Figure 4-3: SARA Planning Process, Table 4-2: CompStat Integration, and read the Case Study: Staff Strategy

Meeting. Develop a plan for the next meeting that synchronizes and integrates: (1) ILP, POP, SARA, and CompStat to solve the case study.

## Practical Exercise: Chapter 5

A mid-size police department operates with a small Intelligence Unit cloaked in secrecy. Internal security is very tight, and the exchange of intelligence between intelligence and crime analysts is minimal. The trust factor is absent, and communication and feedback dysfunctional. Moreover, there is little intelligence sharing with other law enforcement agencies.

The Chief of Police requests you to write an internal memorandum, including recommendations, to improve internal and external communications. Refer to Chapter 6, Tables 5-2 to 5-6 on the Johari Window, and Figure 5-2 RTCC Software Arsenal to Analyze Information. Your response and remedial recommendations should not exceed five pages.

## Practical Exercise: Chapter 6

You are a member of the Hometown City Police Department, which is restructuring its planning process. The new ILP architecture is in favor of centralized planning and synchronization of the planning process.

You are presently serving as the Commander of Field Operations and are responsible for briefing the Chief of Police. Gather committee recommendations and prepare the oral briefing in PowerPoint format.

The emphasis will be on targeting an open-air drug market. Review and respond to the case study in Chapter 6 for the basic scenario of the open-air drug market problem.

Develop a centralized planning model that coordinates ILP, COP, POP, and CompStat operations. Apply the Intelligence Cycle Target Centric Approach to open-air drug market solutions.

The seven points of planning linkage in Chapter 6 are helpful points of articulation. Refer to Table 6-2: Intelligence Planning Synchronization, Figure 6-1: Six Points of Planning Linkage, and Figure 6-2: Intelligence Cycle to assess planning requirements.

## Practical Exercise: Chapter 7

Recently, the need has developed in your hometown police agency for a crime analyst position. In lieu of hiring someone in the future, the chief has requested that you write the crime bulletins, until they fill the vacancy.

The written assignment includes a one-page crime bulletin concerning a series of burglaries occurring in the south side of the city.

Refer to Chapter 7 for the appropriate concepts and procedures, especially Figure 7-1: Analytical Timeframe Products, and Figure 7-3: Crime Bulletin Example.

## Practical Exercise: Chapter 8

Vietnamese street gangs terrorize local merchants and engage in extortion. Hometown City has a Vietnamese population of considerable size. Two gangs operate relatively free of law enforcement intervention because the local population is fearful of retaliation. In addition, the police department operates with cultural and language barriers.

The gangs have 20-30 members, and engage in gang warfare and street violence. They are in their early teens and twenties, defraud merchants by borrowing money, and never pay the loan back. Other gang members run a big restaurant bill and walk out without paying the bill.

Some are more direct and use threats to extort protection pay-offs. Others are more direct about their participation in narcotics trafficking, burglaries, armed robberies, and assaults. These young men have drug habits to support, and law-abiding citizens must pay for their addiction.

Write a Strategic Assessment Report of approximately five pages, as described in Chapter 7 and list the charting techniques listed in Chapter 8. Review Chapter 8; identify the methods of analytical charting and models, which assist in this form of organized gang activity.

Refer to Table 8-3 & 8-4: CPTD Model and OCDS Study, Figure 8-3 Drug Cartel Investigations, and Figure 8-5: Cocaine Commodity Flow Analysis for an overview of investigative strategies. Specifically, event flow analysis, association analysis, commodity flow analysis, and VIA charting techniques provide pertinent intelligence for investigation and prosecution.

## Practical Exercise: Chapter 9

Review the case study on Russian Organized Crime (ROC) in Chapter 9, and develop the intelligence protocols. Develop the analytical strategies for conspiracy crimes, (1) informants, (2) undercover operations, (3) physical surveillance tactics, (4) electronic surveillance procedures.

Review Figure 9-1: Informant Management Program, Figure 9-2: Deep Cover Planning, Figure 9-3: Russian Enterprise Structure, and Table 9-2: Russian Illegal Markets.

You have a new assignment as intelligence analyst in the Vice, Organized Crime Unit. Describe how you would coordinate the Intelligence-Led Policing management issues and the role of analytical intelligence requirements. In short, organize the case analysis and investigative intelligence resources. Organize a PowerPoint presentation for the Commander of the Investigative Bureau.

## Practical Exercise: Chapter 10

Recently, you received a promotion to lieutenant. A terrorist bombing emergency requires your response to an unfolding scenario. The tactical responsibilities fall under your supervision, as field commander, and emergency response teams are en route to the unfolding incident.

Refer to the Case Study: Terrorist Simulation in Chapter 10 for a description of the scenario. Read Chapter 10 including: (1) basic threat analysis equation, (2) counterterrorism planning, and (3) plan the tactical response. Review Figure 10-1: Antiterrorism and Counterterrorism Models and the unit on tactical leadership.

Review the crisis management planning, EOP and IAP emergency response portions of the text. Describe the tactical leadership style. Your responsibility is to develop a field incident action plan (IAP). The verbal briefing will include mission orders, tactical emergency plan, logistical plan, and emergency command post (CP).

## Practical Exercise: Epilogue

Review basic Intelligence-led Policing conceptual formulas and prepare to apply them in your law enforcement career. The concepts are flexible; agencies will evaluate, modify, and apply necessary requirements. The equations offer a theoretical basis and framework for critical thinking, strategic and tactical applications.

## Conclusion

Why bother to participate in interactive practical case studies? The answer: active learning and critical thinking enhance knowledge potential. Active learning prepares officers for promotion exams, but more importantly, superior field performance. Passing academic tests is only the beginning of a successful career; field performance earns the respect of followers and superiors.

## Notes

# Appendix A
# Seminar: Intelligence-Led Policing

| | |
|---|---|
| Seminar Description | 101 |
| Course Objectives | 102 |
| Seminar Methods | 102 |
| Teaching Philosophy | 104 |
| Learning Instruction | 104 |
| Evaluation and Learning Process | 104 |
| Attendance | 105 |
| Course Requirements | 106 |

## Seminar Description

Intelligence-led policing (ILP) is the new architecture for managing intelligence in police organizations. The ILP philosophy is oriented toward internal and external intelligence coordination. ILP emphasizes the centralization of intelligence resources and proper dissemination and sharing of police intelligence. The ILP management philosophy advocates applying a critical thinking approach to strategic and tactical strategies. The intelligence cycle assists police leaders in making the best possible decisions with respect to crime control strategies in a democratic society.

Instructional methods focus on the active learning and writing strategies. The case study method and learning simulations offer opportunities for critical thinking and problem-solving applications. Active learning simulations provide opportunities for meaningful group activities that foster critical thinking and criminal justice theoretical applications. This method of criminal justice instruction attempts to initiate an active learning approach that applies: (1) critical thinking; (2) problem-solving; (3) decision-making, and (4) theory and skill applications across the criminal justice curriculum. The basic pedagogy of active learning emphasizes a cooperative classroom climate in which students learn from each other.

## Textbook

Thomas E. Baker, Intelligence-Led Policing: Leadership, Strategies, and Tactics (New York, New York: Looseleaf Law Publications, Inc., 2009).

## Course Objectives

This course presents a general view of ILP from the police leader's point of view. The emphasis is on the role of ILP and intelligence and crime analysis in police decision-making. Upon completion of the course, the student will have a basic understanding of the advanced intelligence gathering process. The basic intelligence cycle and analyst skills assist in the creation of actionable intelligence. Strategic, tactical, and operational intelligence products receive special considerations.

## Seminar Methods

The Intelligence-Led Policing course offers a role-playing and applied laboratory approach that can create opportunities for active learning and application of knowledge gained in other courses. This course considers appropriate intelligence procedures concerning criminal investigations. This computer-enhanced course includes case studies, and practical learning simulations. The ILP writing assignments focus on the production of learner intelligence products.

### Progression 1: The Case Study Method

The case study method has been widely used in the study of law and other academic disciplines. Case studies assist in the student active learning process. Moreover, the case study method allows diverse opinions, critical thinking, and problem-solving.

The learning simulation as a teaching approach is active learning oriented; as a "general concept" referring to constructing and operating on a model that replicates behavioral processes, i.e., learning simulations.

Students learn by playing the role; they learn by internalizing the norms and role requirements.

What are some advantages of learning simulations and related role-playing? The motivational thrust obtained from simulations, critical and problem-solving remains the goal.

## Progression 2: Master Intelligence Concepts

The learners will internalize the basic concepts of intelligence gathering process. They will apply the intelligence cycle to open sources of information. The concept development will include PowerPoint presentations, Internet applications, website bases education, and intelligence software applications.

## Progression 3: Critical Thinking

The learners will be responsible for completing ten verbal and written intelligence product assignments. Refer to the instructional assignments listed in the chapter headings in this course outline.

Why bother to participate in interactive practical case studies? The answer: active learning and critical thinking enhance knowledge potential. Active learning prepares officers for promotion exams, but more importantly, superior field performance. Passing academic tests is only the beginning of a successful career; field performance earns the respect of followers and superiors.

## Progression 4: Follow-Up

It is at this stage that the critical thinking and problem-solving advances: (1) identifying central issues; (2) stating the problem; (3) collecting additional data and evidence; (4) recognizing underlying assumptions, and (5) forming the hypothesis. For the next four to six weeks, students' follow-up, complete reports, collect data, and draw conclusions.

## Teaching Philosophy

Intelligence-Led Policing focuses on a humanistic philosophy that considers the whole student and their learning potential. Each learning unit emphasizes an active learning approach that encourages students to maximize their learning potential through the various learning domains.

## Learning Instruction

- Humanistic educational philosophy
- Learning organizing centers that include: (1) PowerPoint lectures, (2) Blackboard Internet Website, (3) Critical thinking groups, (4) Case studies and learning exercises, (5) Instructor goals, (6) Active learning objectives, and (7) Objective and subjective evaluation strategies
- Learning objectives classified within the following taxonomic system: (1) Cognitive, (2) Affective, (3) Social, and (4) Psychomotor domains
- Learning objectives identify a goal, task, performance, or behavioral activity
- Learning objectives ordered on the degree of difficulty and intended learning levels

## Evaluation and Learning Process

The process of evaluation is necessary to determine instructor effectiveness, student learning, and the revisions of course design. Evaluation design includes objective and multiple-choice questions that include problem-solving behaviors. Moreover, the test system includes final exams, take home critical thinking exams and learning exercises. Some objective questions have possible on-line Internet or classroom practice applications. The classroom critical thinking groups offer another point of student participation and evaluation.

The learning process for Intelligence-Led Policing includes organizing centers that develop learning content. The learning centers for each of the chapters include case studies/practical and learning simulations. In summary, the taxonomic system applications include: (1) educational philosophy, (2) organizing centers, (3) instructor goals, (4) active learning objectives, (5) case studies, and (6) learning simulations.

| TEACHING METHODS AND COURSE OUTLINE |
|---|
| • Instructor Goals |
| • Student Active Learning Objectives |
| • Key Concepts and Terms |
| • Active Learning Assignments |
| • Multiple Choice Tests |
| • Blackboard Internet Assignments |
| • Case Study Practice Exercises |
| • Student Critical Thinking and Problem-Solving Groups |
| • Evaluation Strategies |

## Attendance

Oral, written, and performance testing will measure student progress in the course. The instructor follows the University Handbook on the issue of attendance. The policy in the Handbook states that attendance can be mandatory for all students. Absences that exceed one week require exceptional medical reason. This policy applies to all students.

| Grading for the Course | |
|---|---|
| Exam #1 | 10% |
| Exam #2 | 10% |
| Exam #3 | 10% |
| Group Research Project | 70% |
| Practical Exercises | 100% |

In addition, to gain points for participation and projects, the student must not cut in excess of one week or two weeks with written medical excuses. To receive credit for class participation and projects, the students must have a 65% average on examinations. There will be no make-up exams, except in dire emergencies.

Attendance at class is mandatory and recorded. All students in this course are limited to a maximum of three absences. Students with numerous absences will lose credit for the participation portion of the course. Excessive absenteeism may result in a failure for the course or at least, a lowering of the final grade. Excessive/repeated lateness by students is counted as full absences and is disruptive to both the instructor and other class members. Sleeping in class is mentally comparable to being absent. Moreover, to get credit for the course and projects, students must have passing grades on examinations (65% average).

## Course Requirements

- Attend at least 90 percent of all class meetings.
- Prepare assigned readings for class discussion.
- Satisfactory performance on two student examinations; for example, both exams cover both reading assignments and lecture material. The instructional emphasis is on theories and conceptual issues. Exams include multiple-choice items, matching items, and short-answer or essay questions.
- Makeup exams are rare and in only exceptional circumstances (for instance, commitment to a hospital).

The percentage of correct answers for each exam will be averaged to produce final grades. An exam score and average of 90% or above = A; 80 - 89% = B; 70 - 79% = C; 60 - 69% = D; below 65% = F. Plus grades are at the discretion of the instructor and at the mid-point of the above stated averages. Instructor philosophy is an individual preference and provides learner direction.

## Teaching Philosophy

Many instructors prefer the humanistic philosophy that ensures respect for learners and their right to learn. A teaching philosophy is necessary for behavior consistency and is a prerequisite to curriculum design. Whatever the philosophical position, it answers questions concerning learner destination. For example, this focuses on a humanistic philosophy that considers the whole student and their learning potential. Each learning unit and objectives emphasize an active learning approach that encourages students to maximize their learning potential through the various learning domains.

## Seminar Outline - Learning Objectives and Practical Exercises

### A. PROLOGUE: CRITICAL THINKING AND THE INTELLIGENCE ANALYST

1. Intelligence Analyst
2. Crime Analyst
3. Criminal Investigative Analyst
4. Critical Thinking
5. Professional Organizations
6. Ethical Responsibilities
7. Intelligence Sharing
8. Strategic Leadership and Vision
9. Ten Basic Intelligence Strategies

## Learning Objectives

- List the intelligence analyst responsibilities.
- List crime analyst the responsibilities.
- Describe the management of intelligence operations.
- List key skill requirements for intelligence analysts.
- Identify the intelligence professional organizations.
- Distinguish the connection between critical thinking and intelligence analysis.
- Connect the intelligence relationship among the ten coordinating strategies.

## Practical Exercise

The Hometown police department is interested in the process of hiring an Intelligence-Led Policing manager. As the intelligence officer and commanding officer of the unit, your assignment is to write the job description and supervise the hiring process.

Refer to the PROLOGUE, Table P-1: Staff Requirements and Figure P-1: NCIP'S Recommendations for Guidance. Include your own observations in the written assignment.

### B. CHAPTER 1: INTELLIGENCE-LED POLICING

1. Intelligence-Led Policing Defined
2. Intelligence Analysis Defined
3. Intelligence Cycle Foundations
4. Global Intelligence Working Group
5. Strategic Analysis Strategies
6. Threat Assessment Strategies

## Learning Objectives

- Define the role of intelligence analysis.
- Differentiate between ILP and intelligence analysis.
- Describe the Intelligence-Led Policing model.
- Describe the United Kingdom's National Intelligence model.

- Distinguish the elements of the Intelligence Cycle.
- List the elements of determining order of analysis.
- Identify the six-step process to intelligence dissemination.
- Identify open and covert sources of information.
- Identify threat assessment strategies.
- Identify the role of premonitories.
- Define aggressive analysis.
- Define intelligence estimate.
- Describe the assessment process.
- List the right to privacy legal protections.
- Identify the value of intelligence sharing.
- Identify the elements of the National Intelligence Sharing Plan.

## Practical Exercise

Recently, your police assignment changed from the Homicide Unit to the Intelligence Unit. This is a temporary assignment until a civilian can replace you. You have the responsibility of writing a strategic intelligence estimate on two motorcycle gangs currently operating in your community: Pagans and Warlocks.

These gangs have notorious reputations for activities that include: (1) illegal drugs, (2) prostitution, assault, and murder. The most important consideration is their influence in drug trafficking.

Write a strategic intelligence estimate, approximately ten pages in length. Refer to the Jamaican Posse case study in chapter one for an illustration. Address the following intelligence concepts: (1) threat assessment process, (2) aggressive analysis, (3) and vulnerability analysis.

Apply the Intelligence Cycle to open sources and refer to Chapter 1, Table 1: Threat Analysis Strategies, Figure 1-3: Intelligence Six-Step Process to Dissemination, and Figure 1-2: Intelligence Cycle.

## C. CHAPTER 2: ORGANIZATIONAL STRATEGIES

1. Reorganization
2. Policing Strategies: Synchronization
3. COP Philosophy Coordination

4. POP Coordination
5. CompStat Coordination
6. Focused Policing
7. The New Architecture
8. Blended Holistic Paradigm

## Learning Objectives

- Describe Intelligence-Led Policing from a management perspective.
- List the elements of the COPPS equation.
- List the elements of COPPS, ILP, and CompStat formula.
- Describe the core elements of Community-oriented Policing.
- Describe the elements of Problem-oriented Policing.
- Describe the elements of CompStat.
- Identify elements of CompStat leadership strategies.
- Describe the assessment and effectiveness of leadership strategies.
- List the levels of police intelligence.
- Identify the elements of the new police intelligence architecture.
- Appraise the value of a synchronized holistic or blended paradigm.

## Practical Exercise

The Chief of Police, Commander of Staff and Administration Bureau, and Intelligence Commander are in the process of developing the new architecture for Intelligence-Led Policing. The Central Planning Committee has requested that you provide an organizational chart that blends and synchronizes: (1) Community-oriented Policing (COP), Problem-oriented Policing (POP), CompStat operations, and ILP.

The goal is to integrate independent operations under the ILP architecture. The new organizational chart would reflect the centralization of overlapping functions.

Submit this one-page chart based upon the content in Chapter 2, Table 2-2: Problem-oriented Policing, Table 2-3: CompStat Leadership Strategies, Table 2-5: Levels of Intelligence, Table 2-6: Blended Holistic Paradigm, and Figure 2-2: New Architecture.

## D. CHAPTER 3: CRIME ANALYSIS STRATEGIES

1. Crime Analysis Strategies
2. Criminal Analysis
3. Strategic Analysis
4. Tactical Analysis
5. Administrative Analysis
6. Operations Analysis
7. Tactical Planning
8. Tactical Crime Linkage
9. Patrol Deployment Operations
10. GIS Crime Mapping

## Learning Objectives

- Define crime analysis.
- Define strategic intelligence.
- Define tactical intelligence.
- Define administrative analysis.
- Define operations analysis.
- Describe the tactical planning process.
- List the elements of profile analysis.
- Identify the elements of target selection.
- Define the function of statistics in police deployment and operations.
- Describe the function of geographical analysis in police operations.
- Identify the function of tactical crime linkage.
- Distinguish the following crime linkage terms: pattern, trend, series, spree, hotspot, hot product, and hot target.
- Describe Geographic Information Systems (GIS) applications to crime analysis.
- List the research applications for crime mapping.
- Identify the elements of crime mapping tactical analysis.

## Practical Exercise

You serve as the crime analyst for the new ILP Unit. The Commander requests a tactical analysis report of the recent series of community bank robberies. The goal is to develop tactical planning strategies for the purpose of prevention and intervention. The report length should be approximately five pages.

Refer to Chapter 3, and examine the key concepts: (1) target profile analysis, (2) statistical analysis, (3) and geographical analysis. Read the Case Study Example, The Analyst Briefing, for an example of the application of basic crime analysis concepts. In addition, refer to Table 3-2: Modus Operandi Criteria, Table 3-2a: Trademark Behaviors, and Figure 3-1: Generalizations Applications to the Use of Maps.

## E. CHAPTER 4: COMPSTAT OPERATIONS

1. ILP Synchronization
2. POP Integration
3. SARA Planning Model
4. CompStat Integration
5. CompStat Strategies

## Learning Objectives

- Distinguish the role of POP and SARA in the planning process.
- Describe the SARA planning model.
- List the SARA planning stages.
- Identify the elements of CompStat.
- Identify the steps for integrating CompStat leadership requirements.
- Identify the role of intelligence requirements for POP and CompStat.
- Identify the need for crime pattern information.
- Describe the value of integrated police strategies.

## Practical Exercise

A series of commercial burglaries have recently plagued Hometown City. The burglars attack small and large retail stores in the downtown areas. They also include neighborhood stores, restaurants, and gas stations. More recently, the pattern has change to a local national banking service.

As the commander of the research unit, you are responsible for the POP planning and CompStat coordination. Describe how Intelligence-

Led Policing plays a significant part of centralization of intelligence and crime analysis to support this robbery problem.

Refer to Chapter 4, Figure 4-1: ILP Integration Strategies, Figure 4-2: ILP Communication and Feedback, Figure 4-3: SARA Planning Process, Table 4-2: CompStat Integration, and read the Case Study: Staff Strategy Meeting. Develop a plan for the next meeting that synchronizes and integrates: (1) ILP, POP, SARA, and CompStat to solve the case study.

### F. CHAPTER 5: STRATEGIC LEADERSHIP AND COMMUNICATION

1. ILP Information Sharing Requirements
2. Communication Feedback
3. Leadership and Vision
4. ILP Mission Statement
5. Johari Window Concepts
6. NYPD's Real Time Crime Center

## Learning Objectives

- Distinguish the relationship between leadership and vision.
- List the elements of a mission statement for Intelligence-Led Policing.
- Describe an overview of the Johari Window Model.
- Define the following Johari Window terms: hidden area, public area, blind area, and unknown.
- Describe the feedback concept.
- Identify the Johari Window Model's relationship to police strategic leadership.
- Identify the value of the Johari Window in the intelligence sharing process.
- Identify the Johari Window function concerning field operations applications.
- Describe the value of the NYPD's Real Time Crime Center (RTCC).

## Practical Exercise

A mid-size police department operates with a small Intelligence Unit cloaked in secrecy. Internal security is very tight, and the exchange of intelligence between intelligence and crime analysts minimal. The trust factor is absent, and communication and feedback dysfunctional. Moreover, there is little intelligence sharing with other law enforcement agencies.

The Chief of Police requests you to write an internal memorandum, including recommendations, to improve internal and external communications. Refer to Chapter 6, Tables 5-2 to 5-6 on the Johari Window, and Figure 5-2 RTCC Software Arsenal to Analyze Information. Your response and remedial recommendations should not exceed five pages.

## G. CHAPTER 6: LEADERSHIP AND PLANNING

1. Leadership and Police Planning
2. Strategic Planning
3. Planning Synchronization
4. Centralized Planning
5. Planning Articulation
6. Emergency Planning
7. Fusion Centers
8. Targeting Coordination
9. Target-Centric Approach

## Learning Objectives

- Define the role of police planning in the ILP management process.
- List the goals of effective planning.
- Define strategic planning.
- Define the term "operational intelligence planning."
- Describe the synchronization of the planning process.
- Describe the need for centralized planning.
- List the elements of the strategic planning process.
- List the six points of planning linkage.
- Identify the role of Emergency Operations Planning (EOP).

- Define the elements of an Incident Action Plan (IAP).
- Identify the role of timing in the planning process.
- Describe the role of fusion centers.
- List the elements of the intelligence cycle planning.
- Describe the intelligence targeting process.
- Define the vital intelligence elements of the Target Centric Approach.
- List the elements of the crime triangle.
- Describe the target selection information and selection process.

## Practical Exercise

You are a member of the Hometown City Police Department, which is restructuring its planning process. The new ILP architecture is in favor of centralized planning and synchronization of the planning process.

You are presently serving as the Commander of Field Operations and are responsible for briefing the Chief of Police. Gather committee recommendations and prepare the oral briefing in PowerPoint format.

The emphasis will be on targeting an open-air drug market. Review and respond to the case study in Chapter 6 for the basic scenario of the open-air drug market problem.

Develop a centralized planning model that coordinates ILP, COP, POP, and CompStat operations. Apply the Intelligence Cycle Target Centric Approach to open-air drug market solutions.

The seven points of planning linkage in Chapter 6 are helpful points of articulation. Refer to Table 6-2: Intelligence Planning Synchronization, Figure 6-1: Six Points of Planning Linkage, and Figure 6-2: Intelligence Cycle to assess planning requirements.

## H. CHAPTER 7: ANALYTICAL PRODUCTS

1. ILP Management of Analytical Documents
2. Intelligence Products
3. Written Products

4. Verbal Presentations
5. Strategic Products
6. Tactical Products
7. Operational Reporting
8. Field Criminal Information Report
9. Quarterly Trend Reports
10. Strategic Threat Assessment

## Learning Objectives

- Describe the need for intelligence products.
- Describe the elements of a written report.
- Describe the elements of a verbal report.
- List the three main levels of intelligence analysis products.
- List the elements of tactical reporting.
- Identify the elements of operational reporting.
- List the elements of effective dissemination requirements.
- List the seven finished intelligence products.
- Describe the need for superior field intelligence reporting.
- Describe the purpose of the Quarterly Trend Report.
- Describe the purpose of the Strategic Threat Assessment Report.
- Identify the elements of the Warning Report.
- Identify the elements of the Crime Bulletin Report.

## Practical Exercise

Recently, the need has developed in your hometown police agency for a crime analyst position. In lieu of hiring someone in the future, the chief has requested that you write the crime bulletins, until they fill the vacancy.

The written assignment includes a one-page crime bulletin concerning a series of burglaries occurring in the south side of the city.

Refer to Chapter 7 for the appropriate concepts and procedures, especially Figure 7-1: Analytical Timeframe Products, and Figure 7-3: Crime Bulletin Example.

## I. CHAPTER 8: ANALYTICAL MODELS AND CHARTING

1. ILP Reporting Requirements
2. Models
3. IALEIA Standards
4. Pattern Analysis
5. Analytical Charting

## Learning Objectives

- Describe the need for analytical intelligence reporting.
- Describe the need for analytical model products.
- Describe the need for analytical charting products.
- List the elements of descriptive analytical intelligence reporting.
- List the elements of explanatory analytical intelligence reporting.
- List the elements of predictive analytical intelligence reporting.
- List the elements of pattern analysis.
- Describe the use of Analyst's Notebook computer systems.
- Identify the various basic analytical charting products.
- Identify the need for review and assessment of intelligence reports in the main text.

## Practical Exercise

Vietnamese street gangs terrorize local merchants and engage in extortion. Hometown City has a Vietnamese population of considerable size. Two gangs operate relatively free of law enforcement intervention because the local population is fearful of retaliation. In addition, the police department operates with cultural and language barriers.

The gangs have 20-30 members, and engage in gang warfare and street violence. They are in their early teens and twenties, defrauding merchants by borrowing money, and never paying the loan back. Other gang members run a big restaurant bill and walk out without paying the bill.

Some are more direct and use threats to extort protection pay-offs. Others are more direct about their participation in narcotics trafficking, burglaries, armed robberies, and assaults. These young men have drug habits to support, and law-abiding citizens must pay for their addiction.

Write a Strategic Assessment Report of approximately five pages, as described in Chapter 7 and list the charting techniques listed in Chapter 8. Review Chapter 8; identify the methods of analytical charting and models, which assist in this form of organized gang activity.

Refer to Table 8-3 & 8-4: CPTD Model and OCDS Study, Figure 8-3 Drug Cartel Investigations, and Figure 8-5: Cocaine Commodity Flow Analysis for an overview of investigative strategies. Specifically, event flow analysis, association analysis, commodity flow analysis, and VIA charting techniques provide pertinent intelligence for investigation and prosecution.

## J. CHAPTER 9: INVESTIGATIVE STRATEGIES

1. Enterprise Conspiracy Crimes
2. Conspiracy Crimes Defined
3. Management of Informants
4. Undercover Operations
5. Physical Surveillance
6. Electronic Surveillance

## Learning Objectives

- List the key basic tools for investigating complex conspiracy crimes.
- Define HUMINT.
- Define COMINT.
- Define the enterprise concept from an enforcement perspective.
- List the types of crimes that fall under the enterprise crime theory.
- Define the elements of the crime of conspiracy.
- Describe the elements of the Informant Management Program.
- Describe the elements of successful law enforcement undercover operations.
- List the elements of deep cover planning.
- Identify the elements of undercover operations planning.
- Define the two basic types of physical surveillance.
- Describe the strategies of the A-B-C surveillance system.

- List the basic provisions of electronic surveillance.
- Define the term pen-register.
- Define telephone analysis.
- Define financial analysis.
- Describe the need for review and assessment of intelligence reports in the main text.

## Practical Exercise

Review the case study on Russian Organized Crime (ROC) in Chapter 9, and develop the intelligence protocols. Develop the analytical strategies for conspiracy crimes, (1) informants, (2) undercover operations, (3) physical surveillance tactics, (4) electronic surveillance procedures.

Review Figure 9-1: Informant Management Program, Figure 9-2: Deep Cover Planning, Figure 9-3: Russian Enterprise Structure, and Table 9-2: Russian Illegal Markets.

You have a new assignment as intelligence analyst in the Vice, Organized Crime Unit. Describe how you would coordinate the Intelligence-Led Policing management issues and the role of analytical intelligence requirements. In short, organize the case analysis and investigative intelligence resources. Organize a PowerPoint presentation for the Commander of the Investigative Bureau.

### K. CHAPTER 10: TACTICAL LEADERSHIP TRAINING

1. ILP Requirements
2. Antiterrorism v. Counterterrorism Strategies
3. Intelligence Analyst: Terrorism
4. Proactive Terrorism Strategies
5. Threat Analysis
6. Crime Prevention Surveys
7. Crisis Management Planning
8. Crisis Training Strategies
9. Tactical Leadership

## Learning Objectives

- Define antiterrorism.
- List the three antiterrorism planning strategies.
- Define counterterrorism responsibilities.
- List the elements of counterterrorism planning.
- Describe the role of the intelligence analyst in the terrorism assignment.
- Define the intelligence biographical sketch.
- Define the terrorist group profile.
- List the five interconnected processes that are essential to understanding terrorism.
- Identify the need for police operations security.
- Define INFOSEC.
- Define police physical security.
- Define police personal security.
- Define the term threat analysis.
- List the elements of the threat analysis equation.
- Describe the purpose of the crime prevention survey.
- List the first two components in the first phase of the antiterrorism program.
- Identify the essential elements of crisis management planning.
- Describe the basic field planning objectives.
- Define the term goal.
- Define the term objective.
- Explain the role of tactical leadership.
- Identify the four basic styles of NIJ police supervision.
- Identify the best NIJ leadership style for frontline tactical missions.
- Describe the need for review and assessment of intelligence reports in the main text.

## Practical Exercise

Recently, you received a promotion to lieutenant. A terrorist bombing emergency requires your response to an unfolding scenario. The tactical responsibilities fall under your supervision as field commander, and emergency response teams are en route to the unfolding incident.

Refer to the Case Study: Terrorist Simulation in Chapter 10 for a description of the scenario. Read Chapter 10 including: (1) basic threat analysis equation, (2) counterterrorism planning, and (3) plan the tactical response. Review Figure 10-1: Antiterrorism and Counterterrorism Models and the unit on tactical leadership.

Review the crisis management planning, EOP and IAP emergency response portions of the text. Describe the tactical leadership style. Your responsibility is to develop a field incident action plan (IAP). The verbal briefing will include mission orders, tactical emergency plan, logistical plan, and emergency command post (CP).

## L. EPILOGUE: TEN INTELLIGENCE-LED POLICING STRATEGIES

1. Strategic Leadership
2. Intelligence-Led Policing
3. Removing the Barriers
4. Synchronization of COP & POP
5. Strategic Planning
6. Intelligence Analysis
7. Crime Analysis
8. Criminal Investigative Analysis
9. Analytical Reporting
10. Intelligence Sharing

## Learning Objectives

- Identify the ten basic articulated strategies of the text.
- Describe the central planning model.
- Identify the element of Intelligence-Led Policing.
- Identify Intelligence-Led Policing strategic planning model.
- Describe the basic components of Intelligence-Led Policing synchronization.
- List the four formulas that support the "Grand Theory" of ILP.
- Describe the need for review and assessment of intelligence reports in the main text.

## Practical Exercise

Review basic Intelligence-led Policing conceptual equations and prepare to apply them in your law enforcement career. The concepts are flexible; agencies will evaluate, modify, and apply necessary requirements. The equations offer a theoretical basis and framework for critical thinking, strategic and tactical applications.

## CONCLUSION

Critical thinking, active learning, and role-playing are mutually reinforcing conceptual approaches. Learners have diverse learning styles, varied learning strategies help develop more opportunities to access those individuals. Active instructional methods that address the learners' affective, social, and cognitive domains have the potential to influence positive outcomes. Finally, instructors must take responsibility for classroom leadership and accomplishing those learning objectives.

# Appendix B
# Fill in the Blank Questions - Answer Key

| Prologue | |
|---|---|
| P-1. Intelligence | P-4. IALEIA |
| P-2. Crime | P-5. vision |
| P-3. Criminal investigate analysis | P-6. ILP |

| Chapter 1 | |
|---|---|
| 1-1. ILP | 1-6. Judgment and assessment |
| 1-2. cycles | 1-7. GIWG |
| 1-3. overt, covert | 1-8. Strategic intelligence |
| 1-4. Reasonable suspicion | 1-9. Premonitories |
| 1-5. Need to know, security clearance | 1-10. Aggressive analysis |

| Chapter 2 | |
|---|---|
| 2-1. ILP | 2-6. crime analysis, statistical analysis, focused patrol |
| 2-2. Quality | 2-7. Leadership |
| 2-3. ILP | 2-8. Focused policing |
| 2-4. COP philosophy, and ILP | 2-9. Offender, victim, location |
| 2-5. POP | 2-10. ILP |

## Chapter 3

3-1. strategic, tactical, administrative, operations
3-2. Crime analysis
3-3. Crime analysis, intelligence analysis, criminal investigative analysis
3-4. Strategic analysis
3-5. Tactical crime analysis
3-6. Administrative analysis
3-7. Operations analysis
3-8. Target profile, target selection, statistical analysis
3-9. Target profile
3-10. Statistical analysis
3-11. pattern
3-12. Trend
3-13. spree
3-14. serial
3-15. spot
3-16. dot
3-17. Product
3-18. target
3-19. Boost, flag
3-20. Offender, suitable targets, absence of capable guardians
3-21. map, clock, calendar
3-22. Crime mapping

## Chapter 4

4-1. Herman Goldstein
4-2. scanning, analysis, response, assessment
4-3. CompStat
4-4. CompStat
4-5. Predict, prevent
4-6. Failure, planning
4-7. Strategies, tactical, and statistical
4-8. commanders/middle managers
4-9. evolutionary, revolutionary
4-10. Local, regional, state, federal

## Chapter 5

5-1. knowledge, unknown
5-2. Share
5-3. feedback
5-4. trust
5-5. feedback
5-6. effectiveness
5-7. blind spot, unknown
5-8. hidden area
5-9. blind spot, unknown
5-10. open
5-11. verbal, nonverbal
5-12. real-time
5-13. real-time
5-14. data, data analysis
5-15. spotlight
5-16. accurate future assessment
5-17. blind, unknown

## Chapter 6

6-1. Strategic long term
6-2. Strategic intelligence
6-3. statistical analysis
6-4. synchronization
6-5. Planning
6-6. goals, objectives
6-7. EOP
6-8. emergency
6-9. terrorist, tactical
6-10. incident
6-11. impromptu
6-12. back-step
6-13. Timing
6-14. CompStat
6-15. fusion
6-16. fast
6-17. targeting, communication, feedback
6-18. Targeting
6-19. target centered
6-20. offender, victim, location
6-21. cognitive, mental
6-22. template
6-23. good, poor

## Chapter 7

7-1. crime trends, crimes, and security threats
7-2. reporting
7-3. strategic
7-4. Projections
7-5. profiles, biographies, and confirmation
7-6. Operational
7-7. briefings, spot reports, quarterly trend reports, threat assessments, warnings, crime bulletins, after-action reports
7-8. information
7-9. decision briefing
7-10. confirmation
7-11. spot
7-12. field intelligence
7-13. bullet
7-14. QTR
7-15. Threat
7-16. warning
7-17. bulletins
7-18. After-action report
7-19. Strategic, tactical, operational
7-20. Current

## Chapter 8

8-1. visual
8-2. models, charting
8-3. conspiratorial
8-4. networks
8-5. ten
8-6. Models
8-7. Models, charting
8-8. model
8-9. Oscar Newman
8-10. territorial, natural surveillance, image, milieu
8-11. territorial
8-12. natural surveillance
8-13. milieu
8-14. designing-out
8-15. Notebook
8-16. Event
8-17. Association
8-18. analyzing
8-19. Commodity

## Chapter 9

| | | | |
|---|---|---|---|
| 9-1. | Enterprise | 9-11. | train, survive |
| 9-2. | legal, illegal | 9-12. | drop-zone, field notes |
| 9-3. | globalization | 9-13. | lone-wolf |
| 9-4. | conspiracy | 9-14. | fixed, mobile |
| 9-5. | Informants | 9-15. | A-B-C |
| 9-6. | bread, butter | 9-16. | association, link, market |
| 9-7. | code-number | 9-17. | pen-register |
| 9-8. | top-secret | 9-18. | Vory |
| 9-9. | Undercover | 9-19. | daisy-chain |
| 9-10. | deep | 9-20. | decentralized |

## Chapter 10

| | | | |
|---|---|---|---|
| 10-1. | operations security, personnel security, physical security, crisis management | 10-8. | Operational security |
| | | 10-9. | Threat |
| | | 10-10. | Crime prevention |
| | | 10-11. | Physical security |
| 10-2. | immediate | 10-12. | Crisis |
| 10-3. | Biographical | 10-13. | traditional, active, innovative, supportive |
| 10-4. | biographical | | |
| 10-5. | individuals | 10-14. | traditional |
| 10-6. | proactive, reactive | 10-15. | Frontline |
| 10-7. | Information Security (INFOSEC) | | |

**Epilogue**

E-1. crime
E-2. strategic
E-3. ILP
E-4. Critical thinking
E-5. community, civilian staff, police mission
E-6. diffusion, adoption
E-7. intelligence
E-8. collection, analysis, dissemination
E-9. Crime
E-10. long-term, short-term
E-11. surveys
E-12. crime specific
E-13. heart
E-14. ECHELON
E-15. DCS-1000

# APPENDIX C
# MULTIPLE CHOICE QUESTIONS - ANSWER KEY

| Multiple Choice Questions Appendix "C" | Answer Sheet |
|---|---|
| Prologue<br>1. C<br>2. A<br>3. D<br>4. D<br>5. D | Chapter 6<br>1. E<br>2. A<br>3. B<br>4. B<br>5. C |
| Chapter 1<br>1. D<br>2. C<br>3. C<br>4. B<br>5. D | Chapter 7<br>1. D<br>2. D<br>3. B<br>4. B<br>5. B |
| Chapter 2<br>1. D<br>2. D<br>3. D<br>4. C<br>5. C | Chapter 8<br>1. B<br>2. C<br>3. B<br>4. C<br>5. C |
| Chapter 3<br>1. D<br>2. D<br>3. D<br>4. D<br>5. D | Chapter 9<br>1. C<br>2. C<br>3. B<br>4. B<br>5. C |
| Chapter 4<br>1. D<br>2. A<br>3. C<br>4. C<br>5. A | Chapter 10<br>1. C<br>2. C<br>3. B<br>4. A<br>5. B |
| Chapter 5<br>1. C<br>2. D<br>3. D<br>4. A<br>5. D | Epilogue<br>1. D<br>2. B<br>3. A |

# APPENDIX D
## CRITICAL THINKING ESSAY QUESTIONS

1. Explain the role of Intelligence-Led Policing.

2. Explain the functions of intelligence analysis.

3. Explain the functions of crime analysis.

4. Explain the role of criminal investigative analysis.

5. Explain the steps in the intelligence cycle.

6. Describe the intelligence sharing process.

7. Describe critical thinking in the intelligence gathering process.

8. Describe common types of intelligence sources.

9. Explain the difference between Intelligence-Led Policing and intelligence analysis.

10. Explain the linkage of ILP, COP, POP, and CompStat.

11. Describe the synchronization of a holistic police paradigm.

12. Explain the role of the ILP Intelligence Cycle in police decision-making.

13. Explain principles of enterprise crime.

14. Describe the basic concepts of conspiracy investigation.

15. Discuss the common characteristics of intelligence products.

16. Describe the evidence Intelligence Cycle collection process.

17. Describe intelligence analytical models.

18. Describe the police planning process.

19. Describe principles of emergency planning.

20. Describe the elements of tactical leadership strategies.

### Extremely Difficult: Critical Thinking Questions

21. Explain the importance of identifying the ten basic intelligence strategies.

22. Describe the elements of the "grand theory" of ILP.

# Appendix E
# ILP Instructor: Critical Thinking Exam

1. Your ILP manager requests a compilation of data, which measures historical data. In addition, includes information on drug supply routes, prices, source country, production, availability, and future trends. This information is useful from an interdiction point of view. You select the following approach:

    A. Intelligence analysis
    B. Criminal investigative analysis
    C. Strategic intelligence estimate
    D. None of the above

2. The Commander/Operations Bureau requests a _____ intelligence product that would compile known data on individuals or entities to provide investigators or prosecutors with these data to augment other types of analytical products or methods or to be used alone.

    A. VIA chart
    B. Flow chart
    C. Biographical sketch
    D. None of the above

3. Your ILP Manager requests a strategic intelligence estimate that is a compilation of data, which measures the historical occurrences of criminal activity. The product is often presented as a(n):

    A. Investigative analysis
    B. Forecasts
    C. Premonitories
    D. None of the above

4. Your ILP Manager requires _____ analysis that depicts the relationships among people, in groups, businesses, or other entities, which make available the information on the nature of the group, and the manner in which the group interacts.

   A. Event flow
   B. Commodity flow
   C. Association
   D. All of the above
   E. None of the above

5. Your ILP Manager suggests that you develop an assessment of an enterprise group. You know that there are short-range assessments that bridge the gap between investigative and strategic intelligence. They generate investigative targets. You select a _____.

   A. Premonitory assessment
   B. Strategic assessment
   C. Tactical assessment
   D. None of the above

6. While reviewing some intelligence information, you classify the statement as presumptuous, on the part of the analyst. "Asian organized crime clearly poses a serious threat in many parts of the world, and in some parts of the United States. However, the level of threat may be overstated in recent claims that Asian organized crime will end up being the number one organized crime problem in the next few years, and that Asian groups, will make the Sicilian Mafia look like a bunch of Sunday school kids." This statement best illustrates _____.

   A. Criminal investigative analysis
   B. Intelligence analysis
   C. Strategic assessment
   D. None of the above

7. Your ILP Manager drops the following report on your desk and requests a verbal briefing. Outlaw biker clubs lack the sophistication and are too oriented toward shortsighted hedonism to be highly successful criminal organizations. They lack the connections with law enforcement and/or the political power base to be major players in organized crime. They appear severely weakened by the successful prosecutions, and they face numerous prosecutions. The above-mentioned paragraph best describes _____.

    A. Profile
    B. Modus operandi
    C. Strategic assessment
    D. None of the above

8. ILP manager has requested a study of long-term trends that may take the form of a quarterly or eventually an annual report. _____ is the proper format to follow.

    A. Strategic analysis
    B. Tactical analysis
    C. Crime analysis
    D. None of the above

9. The ILP team is attempting an intervention in a burglary ring investigation. Crime analysis uncovers a distinct pattern. _____ is the best enforcement course of action.

    A. Strategic analysis
    B. Tactical analysis
    C. Criminal investigative analysis
    D. None of the above

10. The Commander and ILP manager requests _____ information on patrol practices. The analysis and information assists police leaders in planning patrol allocation and logistical support.

    A. Operations analysis
    B. Strategic analysis
    C. Tactical analysis
    D. None of the above

# ANSWER SOLUTION KEY

1. C
2. A
3. B
4. C
5. A
6. C
7. C
8. A
9. B
10. A

# Notes

## OTHER TITLES OF INTEREST
## FROM LOOSELEAF LAW PUBLICATIONS, INC.

Effective Police Leadership, 2nd Edition
    by Thomas E. Baker

Test Preparation and Seminar Guide for Effective Police Leadership
    by Thomas E. Baker

Effective Police Leadership Training Powerpoint Presentation
    *Available upon request for instructors*
    by Thomas E. Baker

What Every Chief Executive Should Know
    by Jon M. Shane

Developing the Survival Attitude
    by Phil L. Duran

A Practical Career Guide for Criminal Justice Professionals
    by Michael Carpenter and Roger Fulton

Building a Successful Law Enforcement Career
    *Common-Sense Wisdom for the New Officer*
    by Ryan E. Melsky

Constitutional Police Procedure, *An Instructional Dialogue*
    by Michael A. Petrillo

Conflict Resolution for Law Enforcement, *Street-Smart Negotiating*
    by Kyle E. Blanchfield, Thomas A. Blanchfield, and Peter D. Ladd

The Verbal Judo Way of Leadership
    *Empowering the Thin Blue Line from the Inside Up*
    by Dr. George Thompson & Gregory A. Walker

    (800) 647-5547        www.LooseleafLaw.com